SOUNDS IRISH

THE IRISH LANGUAGE IN AUSTRALIA

Dymphna Lonergan was born in Dublin, Ireland, where she studied the Irish language in school. She immigrated to Australia in 1972. In 1994 she was awarded a Masters degree by Flinders University of South Australia for her study of Irish language words in Anglo-Irish writing. She was awarded a PhD from Flinders in 2002 for her thesis on 'The Irish language in Australia'. Currently teaching in the English department at Flinders, she continues to research the Irish influence on Australian English. Other interests include conversing in Irish in Adelaide, and attending annual daonscoileanna (folkschools) in Melbourne and Sydney.

SOUNDS IRISH

THE IRISH LANGUAGE IN AUSTRALIA

Dymphna Lonergan

[COUNTRY AND LANGUAGE FOREVER]

LYTHRUM PRESS
ADELAIDE

First published by

Lythrum Press
128 Hindley Street, Adelaide
South Australia 5000
www.lythrumpress.com.au

October 2004

Front cover design by Irene Previn
Cover photographs: sculpture by John Lonergan
Book designed and typeset by Michael Deves
Printed and bound by Hyde Park Press

National Library of Australia
Cataloguing-in-Publication entry
Lonergan, Dymphna.
Sounds Irish: the Irish language in Australia.
Bibliography.
Includes index.
ISBN 1 921013 00 1
1. Irish language – Australia. 2. Irish language – Australia – History.
3. Irish Australians – History. I.Title.

491.620994

Production of this book has been supported by the Australian Academy of the Humanities, and Flinders University of South Australia.

This project has been assisted by the Australian Government through the Australia Council, its arts funding and advisory body.

CONTENTS

Acknowledgements

The idea that I should research the Irish language in Australia came from Emeritus Professor Diarmaid Ó Muirithe of University College Dublin: my thanks to him. The major support for my work, however, came from Flinders University, especially Associate Professor Lyn Jacobs and Professor Graham Tulloch. I am grateful for the financial support towards the publication of this book from Flinders University, The Academy of the Humanities and the Arts Council of Australia.

Working 'out of country' on the Irish language has had obvious disadvantages. These were, nevertheless, far outweighed by the advantages gained in the need to find support and sources in Australia. Thanks must go in the first place to the Irish Australian and Irish language community members nationwide who shared their ideas and family stories with me in emails, at conferences and at Irish language summer schools and winter schools. I would like to name especially Tomás de Bhaldraithe, Gregory Byrnes, Michael Dollard, Patrick Joyce, Eamonn Naughton, Val Noone, Emer O'Donnell, Colin Ryan, Maurice Scanlon, St John Skilton, and Turloch Vaughan for their interest, ideas and suggestions. Thank you to my Australian family and friends, especially my children Kate and Johnny, Mick and Vicki Forrest, and Emer O'Donnell, for their love and support. Thank you to my family in Ireland, my sisters Noreen and Cherie and Elizabeth O'Mahony especially, for their hospitality and ongoing love and friendship. Thank you to my late husband, John, for our thirty years together, *ach mothaim uaim go mór thú, a Sheáin Uí Lonnargáin.*

The publisher acknowledges permission to publish photographs from the following institutions, and the generous assistance of their staff:

Melbourne Diocesan Historical Commission, Catholic Archdiocese of Melbourne
National Library of Australia, Canberra
National Museums and Galleries of Northern Ireland, Welch Collection Ulster Museum, Belfast
State Library of New South Wales, Sydney

Preface

Most people today view Ireland as an English-speaking country. Even if people are aware that Ireland has a native language, there is a sense that the Irish language is something in the past. Outside of Ireland there is little knowledge that the language plays a major part in Irish culture even today. While there may be an ongoing complaint in Ireland that the language is dying, it is constantly being supported through education and the media. Every Republic of Ireland child learns Irish in school from the age of five. Today the internet gives world-wide access to the Irish language through Raidió na Gaeltachta (www.rng.ie), the all-Irish radio program. Irish language television programs can also be accessed through subscription.

The Irish language may be a minority language in English-speaking Ireland, but it is enshrined in the Irish Constitution as 'the first official language' of the country. Despite the fact that comparatively few Irish people in Ireland speak Irish as a daily form of communication, the Irish will not give their native language away. The native language of Ireland has been an unbroken and sustaining force of Irish cultural expression regardless of numbers of speakers at a given time. One contributing factor to the decline of the numbers of Irish speakers was the Great Famine of the 1840s. While Ireland lost around a million of its Irish speakers to emigration, England, America and Australia gained them.

It is a curious fact, however, that in Australia the assumption has been that these Irish speakers managed to lose their language on their way over on the boat, or that certainly when they reached Australian shores the Irish speakers ceased to speak Irish. Such assumptions are not made about other languages. No one would suggest that Italian speakers lost their Italian on the way over, or that they gave it away for English as soon as they landed. We know how long it takes to learn a second language. We take it for granted that Italians, Iranians, Polish, German and other immigrants to Australia will continue to use their native languages within their family group and with friends and acquaintances, even if they acquire fluency in English. The Irish speaker in Australia is no different. While there may not be many native Irish speakers in Australia today, that was not the case in the eighteenth and nineteenth centuries. During the peak periods when the Irish populated Australia the majority of the Irish people spoke Irish. This book sets out to capture that sound in order to better appreciate the world view of the Irish speaker in

Australia, and to bring to the fore a neglected part of Irish Australian heritage.

The Irish speakers in Australia during the eighteenth and nineteenth centuries did not engage in life writing: they have left neither letters nor diaries written in their native tongue. The only way we can hear these historical voices is through English language texts. This book traces Irish language words, phrases and references in Australian newspapers, poetry and novels, and in Australian English. It begins with a discussion of the written evidence we have of Irish speakers in Australia, from convicts to priests. How the Irish brought new words into Australian English is discussed next. Readers will be surprised to learn how some of the most iconic Australian words are revealed to be Irish words in disguise. A glossary of Irish words in Australian writing completes this tour of Irish sounds, and should be of interest to writers and readers alike.

Because my focus was on capturing Irish words in print, I have not discriminated in my source material. Works of clearly high literary value sit alongside popular writing, and I have been as much interested in a letter to a newspaper as in a finely crafted poem. A word about terminology: I use the term *Irish* for the Irish language because that is the English word the Irish use for their native language. In Irish the word is *Gaeilge;* which significantly means speech in general as well as specifically 'Irish'. The term 'Gaelic' may have included the Irish language at one point, but now applies more to Scots Gaelic and is best avoided when referring to the Irish language. Lastly, while there are a number of terms for the English of Ireland, I prefer 'Irish English' over the terms Hiberno English and Anglo-Irish.

Dymphna Lonergan
Adelaide, 2004

The author as a schoolgirl in Dublin

II.—Cúrsaí Tinteáin is Scoile.

Pádraig do ṫeaċt aḃaile. Mar a fuair Seán a leas-ainm. Bean ṁic istiġ. Bás an tSean-ṁáistir Scoile. Múinteoir nua.

UAIR a ḃí na prátaí ite againn, d'imiġ m'aṫair is Seán ag boṫántaíoċt. Ní raiḃ éinne im ṫeannta féin ansan aċ Máire a ḃí ag cniotáil. Níorḃ ḟada gur ṫit mo ċodlaḋ orm. Nuair a ṫáinig m'aṫair aḃaile do ḃíos im ḋúiseaċt. Do ċuala é 'á rá lem ṁáṫair—

"Beiḋ Pádraig ag teaċt aḃaile i gcoṁair an tSaṫairn," ar seisean.

"Ṁuise, dar fia! Dé a ḃeaṫa!" arsa mo ṁáṫair.

Do ġeit mo ċroí le háṫas, mar b'é mo ḋearṫáir Pádraig a ḃí i gceist acu. Ḃí breis is bliain roiṁe sin ó ḃí sé age baile. Do ḃíoḋ sé in aimsir ó ḃí sé dá ḃliain déag d'aois. Dá ḃrí sin cé gur ṁeasa liomsa Seán go mór ná é, toisc é ḃeiṫ timpeall an tí go minic, mar sin féin ḃí fáilte im ċroí agam do Ṗádraig.

D'imiġ cúpla lá agus tráṫnóna Dé Saṫairn ḃuail Pádraig an doras isteaċ. Do riṫeas féin ina ċoinne, agus ṫóg sé in airde ina ḃaclainn me agus do ṗóg mé go ceanúil. Ċuir sé a láṁ ina ṗóca, agus do ṡín ċugam páipéar

14

A page from the author's schoolgirl reader, Peig, *printed in Irish type.*

To Tyler Lee Lonergan,
from her Mamó: go maire tú slán

Chapter One

The Sweetest and Swiftest Tongue

Her name was Bridget (Biddy) Burke, and she left the barony of Clare in Ireland for Queensland in 1880 aboard the *Dunbar Castle*. Like many other rural Irish female migrants of the time, her occupation was listed as 'domestic'. From a few extant letters sent from Brisbane to her home in Balrobuck Beg, we can see that Biddy was a lively, passionate and, at times, homesick young woman.[1] She was also hoping 'see the old sod once more'. She lamented that she could not make friends easily, or as she put it 'make free with any body'. Writing home was one way of connecting with her own people, but even that activity constrained the lively Biddy, who found the act of writing 'the hardest Job to get through'. Bridget migrated with her younger brother, Patrick. He was some comfort to her in her loneliness, especially when they had a 'long yarn of Home'. This long yarn was probably in the Irish language, as the Burke siblings came from the Irish-speaking parish of Annaghdown. They might have spoken English, but for them it was a second language, and they were more comfortable with their native Irish.

Forty years before Bridget and Patrick left Ireland for Queensland, Michael Tierney left Galway for Tasmania. Michael was a convict, a sheep stealer, and his story is typical of many victims of rural poverty in Ireland who resorted to this kind of crime. In Michael's case, however, there is a question mark over just how criminal his act was, given that he was drunk at the time. At his trial (17 June 1844) Michael claimed to have seen the sheep wandering on the road and to have simply driven them home. The newspaper report does not say exactly how Michael Tierney was found to be in possession of Patrick Ryder's sheep, but evidently Ryder brought the charges that sentenced Michael to transportation for ten years.[2] Michael Tierney was unlucky, because people who committed similar or more serious crimes than his were allowed to serve their sentences in Ireland. Michael, however, was unable to

As well as having 'two scars on little finger, left hand' it was noted under 'Marks' that Michael Tierney 'cannot speak English'.

produce a character witness and this was a deciding factor in the judge's decision. At that time prisoners were not allowed to speak in court, and even if Michael's siblings, John, Mary, Nelly and Winifred, were aware of his incarceration and trial, it is unlikely that they would have been allowed to speak for him. Michael was 38 years old and unmarried and was most likely a *spailpín*, an unskilled migratory labourer who, having no land of his own, was obliged to seek work wherever he could find it. Michael would not have stayed long enough at any job for his employer to get to know him. As far as the judge was concerned Michael was just another one of those worthless *spalpeens* (as it is written in English) Irish society was better off without. So Michael was shipped to Australia, no doubt distressed and confused, and he managed to bring enough attention to himself on arrival for his language state to be noticed. While the account of Michael's trial in the *Tuam Herald* makes no mention of it, the Tasmanian convict record states that he could not speak English.[3]

Even though Bridget Burke had many namesakes in Queensland (and there were two on board the *Dunbar Castle*), it may be possible for her descendants to trace her history should they wish to. She kept in touch with Patrick when he went out bush, and she may have been godmother to a child of his. As for Michael Tierney's history in Australia, the 1860 Deaths in the District of Hobart Town register shows that a Michael Tierney died in Hobart on 3 July

1860 DEATHS in the DISTRICT of Hobart Town

No.	When died	NAME and SURNAME.	Sex.	Age.	Rank or Profession.	Cause of Death.	Signature, Description, and Residence of Informant.	When Registered
2285	July 3rd	Mary Barr	female	43 years	House Servant	Fracture of the skull, cause not known..	[illegible] Coroner	3rd August
2286	July 3rd	Michael Tierney	Male	59 years	Milkman	Bursting of an Aneurism left side chest	[illegible] Coroner	3rd August
2287	July 10th	John Grant	Male	30 years	Boatman	Found drowned, no marks of violence	[illegible] Coroner	3rd August
2288								

The record of the death of Michael Tierney, milkman, at 59 years of age.

1860 from 'Burstings of an aneurism left side chest'. His occupation was recorded as 'milkman'. On the same page of that register the death of a Mary Barr is recorded as 'fracture of the skull cause unknown'. Another person was 'found dead in Green Ponds Coach Canoe' and another was 'found dead in a privy'. We get an overall sense that these deaths were unwitnessed as well as being sudden. We can only speculate where Michael Tierney died and whether there were any witnesses to his death who cared about him and who may have shared the sixteen years he spent away from the old sod.

Bridget Burke and Michael Tierney's first language was Irish, but there is little to tell us what their lives were like as they struggled to express themselves and to connect in an English-speaking world. Even in Ireland, the Census language question was not posed until 1850, some years after millions of Irish speakers had died of Famine or migrated to the new worlds. In these more enlightened times, however, we know and care about the importance of first languages in the settlement of new migrants. We can be certain that Bridget and Michael's English difficulties would have impacted significantly on the life they had. Biddy Burke's difficulty in 'making free' with people was compounded by the fact that her deepest thoughts and feelings were best expressed in the Irish language of her formative years. She would only find true expression when she conversed with her brother or with another *gaeilgeoir*. We can imagine Michael Tierney's linguistic isolation in those early years of imprisonment and we would like to think that he found fellow Irish-speaking convicts who would have helped him. Perhaps he learned enough English to take on a milkman's job, or perhaps the job required few verbal skills beyond the odd Australian greeting and cheerful whistling.

The Irish migrant experience has been a frequently reported aspect of Australia's early European history. In particular, the activities of Ireland's

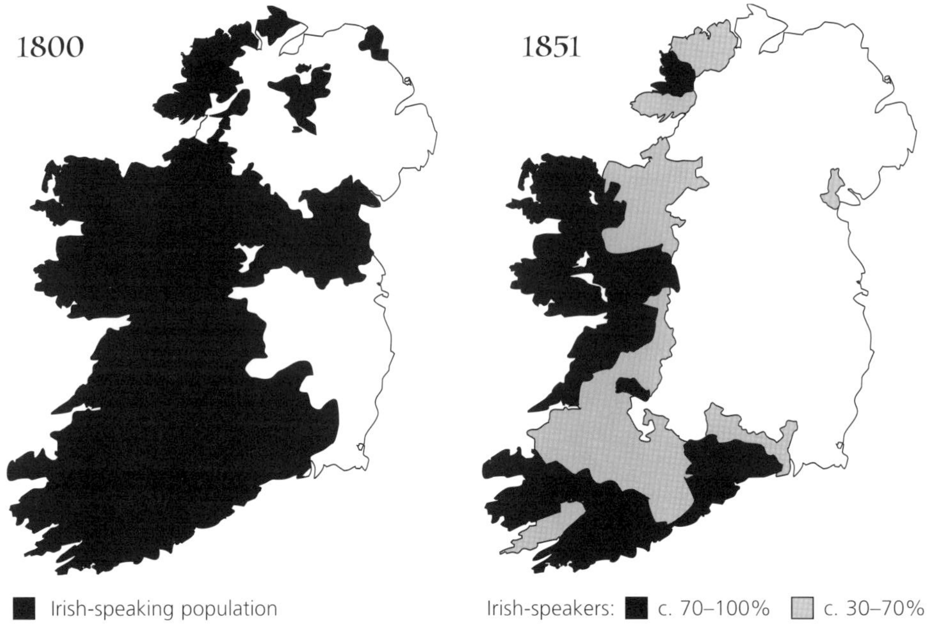

Between 1800 and 1851 the number of Irish speakers in Ireland declined markedly, as a consequence of the Great Famine and emigration.

'unwilling' emigrants – transported convicts – have provided historians with a wealth of material for bringing that period to life. The late eighteenth- and early nineteenth-century Irish in Australia were numerous, and, at various times they were described as being turbulent, dissatisfied, extremely insolent, refractory, ignorant, obstinate, depraved and troublesome. These Irish were at the forefront of both potential and actual revolution in the penal colony, and to the horror of the authorities there were six hundred United Irishmen in the colony by 1801. The Castle Hill uprising of 1804 was led by Irishmen who were willing to accept Death or Liberty over their convict status. These troublemakers were a bad influence on others, including the English convicts.

The Irish were also a notable colonial presence as free migrants. Irish women such as Biddy Burke made up a large proportion of Australia's female domestic servants. The Irish were active in the goldfields and were among the leadership of the Eureka rebellion of miners in 1854, but they generally occupied the lowest classes in the Colony. One commentator went so far as to call them 'the poorest, most useless and most dissolute part of the population'.[4] Overall, the presence of the Irish in Australia ensured that the social order would not be a copy of Home (that is, England). The Irish, whether convicts or free settlers, had a different world view and behaved accordingly.

The fundamental difference that separated the Irish from the English in the Australia of the eighteenth and nineteenth centuries was language, whether in terms of speaking a language other than English or speaking English that was considered to be poor. Socially, politically and culturally, the language you used determined whether you belonged to the dominant group or to a group on the margins. The Irish brogue is a cultural difference even today. Through the traces of Irish language elements extant in the English of Australia we can hear better the stories of Bridget Burke and Michael Tierney. These words and phrases are a collective memory of the Irish in Australia.

While there are a number of native Irish speakers living in Australia today, there are none for whom the Irish language is their only form of expression. This latter case was the situation, however, throughout the late eighteenth and nineteenth centuries for many Irish people who arrived from a non-English speaking background in rural Ireland. While some may have had a command of English, others had little or none. Although Ireland is now viewed as an English-speaking country, this represents a comparatively rapid change from a dominant Irish language to English. The English language was introduced into Ireland in the twelfth century; however, for nine hundred years prior to this and until the end of the nineteenth century Irish was the primary language of many Irish people. For example, in 1845, the year after Michael Tierney left, there were more Irish speakers in the country than at any time in the history of the language.

Shortly after Captain Cook's arrival in Australia, Englishman Arthur Young toured Ireland. Young recorded that he found the English language spoken without any mixture of the Irish language in only two places, in Dublin and in County Wexford.[5] Dublin is where the Irish Parliament sat. These parliamentarians were, in the main, upper middle class, Protestant, land-owning and English-speaking males. Outside of these districts the Irish language was the language of everyday use, although English would also have been used in towns and villages, especially where trade was involved.

The average Irish rural person did not travel far from home. Even today the same surnames can be found in the same areas of the country as they have been for centuries. Those who did leave their homes may have travelled for work, for adventure or for a better life, to the towns and cities of Ireland or abroad. Irish-speaking men could also find themselves suddenly transported thousand of miles away from home as prisoners of one kind or another. Some were caught up in the revolutionary activities of their own country, such as the rebellion of 1798. Others found themselves in foreign armies, whether through choice or through being press-ganged. Irish-speakers were among those who were rounded up following the rebellion of 1798, and one group of about thirty who had no English was mentioned in the diary kept by the captain's wife on board the *Friendship* during the voyage to Australia in 1800.[6]

At that time the authorities saw the use of a language other than English as a threat to their ability to control, and the Irish language was one such threat. Of most concern were the hundreds of Irish political prisoners in the Colony who were there because of the failed 1798 rebellion and who might want to cause similar trouble in Australia. *Anyone* speaking Irish was suspect. In 1800 Hestor Stroud reported her suspicions of Irish speakers at the camp in Toongabby who were walking up and down and talking earnestly in Irish. At their trial in 1800 she said they must have been speaking Irish because they were plotting to stage a rebellion. Perhaps they were, but perhaps they were also having a yarn about home. Outside in the civilian world even the symbolic use of Irish could get you into trouble, as the Rev. James Dixon discovered when he was censured for singing a song containing the phrase *Érin go brách* (Ireland forever), and for wearing a medal which carried the same saying. This phrase has certainly been used as a political rallying cry, but it is also a simple endearment, such as when Biddy Burke wrote 'Queensland for Ever augus un Ballybug go Braugh' at the end of one of her letters home. In this instance Biddy's home *Ballybug* replaces *Érin*.

At the time the Rev. Dixon was singing his patriotic song he was not on official church business in Australia, although he celebrated the first Catholic Mass in Sydney in 1803. Seventeen years passed before the first official Catholic priests arrived, and when they did they found the Irish language in use in Australia. Father O'Neill stepped off the boat in 1803 to be greeted immediately by a woman who spoke to him in Irish asking him if he recognised her from home. Irish Catholics in Australia who only knew how to confess in their native language needed Irish-speaking priests, but, practicalities aside, this sound of home at the end of the world was also a joy to hear. In 1817 one old convict thought that Father Jeremiah O'Flynn's Irish was 'the swiftest and sweetest tongue' he had ever heard.[7] As the old convict had arrived in Australia with Irish alone, we can imagine his delight on hearing his native language once again. These early priests found the Irish language to be an important means of communication between the priest and his parishioners. Even if many of the Irish had learned English at that time, it is likely that they continued to pray in Irish and the ritual of Confession would have been easier to carry out in the language in which it was originally learned. Priests who did not have Irish were handicapped, as Father Therry lamented in 1820. He was supported by Father Connolly, who also wrote home to a priest friend insisting that priests in Australia would be unable to hear confessions unless they were Irish-speaking. In 1824 this was dramatically borne out when this Father Connolly wrote down for the authorities the confession of an Irish-speaking convict before the convict's execution. When Colonial officials saw the written confession they thought the language was Hebrew. A priest's ability to speak the Irish language earned him the respect of others, as Father Francis Moore discovered when he was introduced to the Catholic Association of Melbourne in 1853 as one who was able to address the meeting both in the Queen's language and 'in the fine old Irish tongue'. Another priest, Father Patrick Smyth, a native of Ballina in Ireland living in Ballarat in 1854 was noted for being a Latin and 'Celtic' scholar. Keeping up their language skills in Australia paid off for those who returned home such as the Irish-born Bishop of Lismore who in 1900, on a visit to Ireland, was heard chatting in Irish with the people around Mount Mellory, where he had studied for the priesthood.

It is strange for us to imagine Irish people in Australia unable to speak English or speaking broken English, but this was the situation in the eighteenth and nineteenth century for some. Was it around the same time in Britain that the Irish were labelled as 'stupid'? Is it possible that the labelling of the Irish as stupid through the telling of 'Irish' jokes began when Irish people with little or no English had to move outside the island of Ireland in order to find work? One such joke – 'How to confuse an Irishman: show him two shovels and tell him to take his pick' – certainly demonstrates a language problem for someone with a limited English vocabulary. Today we know that speaking English as a second language does not always correlate with speaking English fluently, and that neither does speaking English fluently correlate with writing English fluently. Writing English, however, was a problem for Father Daniel Power 1826 when his written reports to the Colonial officials prompted the comment that he was 'as conversant with the Irish language as he was deficient in English'. In the transition from Irish to English there were no doubt a variety of stages towards full bilingualism, and the older the learner, the greater the difficulty in making a full transition.

Sometimes it is simply the oddity of expression or the choice of an inappropriate word that reveals a linguistic heritage. Hestor Stroud's testimony at the trial in 1800 resulted in a flogging for United Irishman and Kerry-born Paddy Galvin. Fellow convict General Joseph Holt recorded that Galvin received three hundred lashes without flinching and with courage and defiance. When asked to reveal where the pikes he was supposed to have made were hidden, Galvin replied:

> You may as well hang me now … for you never will get my music from me so.[8]

Russell Ward has credited Galvin with having been a founder of the

Having received three hundred lashes, Paddy Galvin defiantly refused to co-operate with the authorities:
'you may as well hang me now [he says] for you never will get my music from me so'
Recorded by Joseph Holt. STATE LIBRARY OF NSW

Australian tradition of 'indomitable courage in the face of overwhelming odds'. It is likely that Galvin's 'courage' would not have been as apparent without these poetic words recorded by Holt. Galvin's words, however, may only sound poetical because they are evidence of second language acquisition in a developing stage. If we consider the Irish language equivalent of Galvin's words as

Is fearr libh mé a crocadh, mar ní bainfidh sibh ceol as mo bhéalsa mar sin

they would translate directly as: 'You may as well hang me because you won't take music from my mouth so', and we can see that Galvin's phrase 'music from my mouth' mirrors Irish *ceol*, the word for 'music' but which can also be used idiomatically to mean 'talk', e.g. *beidh ceol faoi seo*, 'there'll be talk about this', but which is literally 'there'll be music about this'. At the time of the flogging, Galvin had not been long away from Kerry where his daily communication would have been in Irish. Galvin may have been translating from Irish to English, and this would account for the peculiarly poetic nature of his words in the middle of a traumatic situation. He would have had to suppress his natural tongue for fear of greater punishment. Irish-speaking migrants, even if they had some command of English, would have had to translate from one language to another all they time they were acquiring fluency in English. It is sobering for me to think that an Irish speaker from the *gaeltachtaí* (the Irish-speaking districts) in 1960s Ireland would have had the same exposure to English as I had to French, and had I bumped into him or her on O'Connell Street in Dublin, I, a Dublin jackeen, might have put any reticence in their country speech down to 'culchie' shyness and not to the fact that their native tongue was Irish.

Even if second language fluency is achieved, it is the primary language that carries the deepest level of emotion. In 1833 a British officer in Cork recorded the poignant scene of a man and a woman calling out to each other in Irish, he on the convict hulk and she on the shore. We can imagine a similar scene between Michael Tierney and his siblings in 1844 and Bridget Burke and her family in 1880.

Most of the Irish-convicts sent to Australia, no doubt, learned English over time, but it would always be a secondary and not a primary language. Irish was the language in their minds, hearts and in their souls. Those who could speak and write English, such as the group on the convict ship the *Bohemian* in 1851, found themselves in another role in teaching others on the long journey out. Irish-speaking convicts were also among those who later escaped, some to a life with Aboriginal people. Indeed many Aborigines would have learned Irish as their first European language and may not have been aware that it was a minority language and not the language of most of the invaders. For instance, Irish-speaking Aborigines met the 1839 Thomas Mitchell expedition at the intersection of the Lachlan and the Murrumbidgee rivers. The Irish shared both language and music with the Aborigines, and there are traces of this contact today, such as in a pidginised Irish language song, in New South Wales Pidgin, and a word for 'shoe' from the Irish of the Aran islands that entered the Ngiyampa language.

The Irish rebellions of the eighteenth and nineteenth centuries resulted in Irish-speaking convicts spending a considerable amount of time in Australia. For many rebels from rural Ireland effective communication in an English-speaking world would have been difficult. This was the case as late as 1863 for settlers such as the 343 Irish-speakers on board the *Donald Mackay*. These free settlers spoke in Irish to one another during the voyage but their English was poor. One observer recorded in his diary that when he asked one of the Irishmen whether he had got the hot water for breakfast, the man answered 'I do'.[9] This speaker could have avoided revealing his poor grasp of past and present tense in English had he used the word 'yes'. The Irish language, however, does not have the terms 'yes' and 'no'. These are indicated by repeating the verb either in the negative or the positive.

The large number of Irish-speaking migrants on board the *Donald Mackay* was not unusual, and their strong need for kith and kin resulted in 'chain migration', often involving a chain of siblings or other relatives following one another, just as Biddy and Patrick Burke followed their uncle Martin to Queensland. Sometimes as a result of sponsorship whole families and

Not all Irish immigrants arriving in Australia were poor. These marriageable young ladies arriving in 1886 are well dressed and comparatively affluent.

FROM *VOYAGE AUTOUR DU MONDE PAR LE COMTE DE BEAUVOIR*, PARIS 1878.
NATIONAL LIBRARY OF AUSTRALIA

even entire parishes emigrated. 'The Donegal Relief Group', a Sydney- and Melbourne-based charity that raised money to assist poor Irish families to emigrate, was such a sponsor. Most of these migrants came from the Donegal *Gaeltacht* area, and there was some concern that they may not have had enough English to make good workers. When the *Sapphire* docked in Sydney in May 1859 a deputation from the sponsoring group went on board to see for themselves. A Catholic priest, Father Powell 'admonished' the migrants at length in Irish, no doubt impressing on them the need to speak as much English as possible. The deputation was satisfied that the men spoke English 'more or less perfect', and that only eleven females spoke Irish alone.[10]

Irish migrants to Australia who had no English had probably lived close to their Irish-speaking home. Adult dependent females, unlike males who may have travelled to markets and fairs, may have had little opportunity to use English even if they had acquired it. Poverty and hardship sent even the young into the big world, as happened to Aodh O Domhnaill, who was hired at a fair in Letterkenny in 1867 only to become very homesick until his employer found another Irish-speaker to talk with him. Finding someone to speak Irish with in eighteenth and nineteenth century Australia was an essential part of successful settlement, and close-knit groups would have spoken Irish on a daily basis.

We now have a picture of a large number of Irish people arriving in

Ann (née Colgan) and John Collins from County Tyrone conversed in Irish.
PHOTO COURTESY FATHER BATEMAN, CANBERRA

Australia speaking the Irish language in family groups and with other Irish they might meet. We know that some had no command of English on arrival, and we can speculate that some never made the language shift. The Irish language was common in New South Wales, Victoria and Queensland where the majority of Irish migrants settled. The language was also in South Australia; Charles Hargrave, South Australia's Inspector General of Roads, met many Irish-speaking people working on the roads in the 1890s. Hargrave was an Irish-speaker himself and wrote to South Australia's *Southern Cross* newspaper in 1898 promoting *The Gaelic Journal*, the Gaelic League's bilingual journal. Irish migration to South Australia was significant in the nineteenth century, promoted through The Emigrant Fund, which was founded to assist labourers to migrate to the new state.

While official historical sources often gloss over the details of day-to-day life, family histories can sometimes flesh this out. The Collins family of Victoria has traced the arrival in 1841 of Ann Colgan from County Tyrone and her marriage to John Collins, also from County Tyrone. Ann was about nineteen when she arrived in Australia, and she could not speak English very well, but she and John conversed in 'Gaelic'. Similarly the Cuneen family has documented that ancestors Patrick and Winifred Nolan were farming in Bendigo in the 1850s and that they too conversed in their native tongue. The Nolans also taught their children their prayers in Irish. Here we can see how aspects of the Irish language were passed from generation to generation. The language was also passed down through songs. Shirley Walker has dedicated her book *Roundabout at Bangalow* to 'Eileen Alannah', the name she had given her daughter, but which was originally in the refrain of a song her grandmother used to sing to her. Sometimes a single word may be all that is left of

Dia duit, a Aintín Úna

An Domhnach a bhí ann.

Bhí sé a deich a chlog ar maidin.

Bhí Áine ina suí ag an fhuinneog ag scríobh.

D'fhéach sí amach.

Chonaic sí Aintín Úna ag teacht.

Rith sí amach go dtí an bus.

"Dia duit, a Aintín Úna," arsa Áine.

"Dia is Muire duit, a Áine," arsa Aintín Úna.

Dia duit Dia is Muire duit

30

A recent child's reader – used at adult Irish language classes in Adelaide

this rich Irish language culture in Australia, but the glimpses we get are often enough for us to appreciate what has been lost. A discussion of 'slang' in Adelaide's *Southern Cross* newspaper on 24 May 1935 is one example of this:

> Another word which was in use among the old people in Australia was 'Shinahawn' (sineachan). It means, literally, a little old man. Bounder, perhaps would translate it.

This is likely to be the word *seangán*. It means an 'ant' but is also used to indicate a weak or insignificant person. While some Irish language terms of abuse are common in English (especially in the English of Ireland) *shinahawn* is not one of them. Here is an Irish word that survived in Australian English into the twentieth century and that probably came directly from Irish speakers in Australia. If it was commonplace among old people in Adelaide's Catholic community in the 1930s it may have been used elsewhere. Wherever a people travels the language travels with them and is passed on in a variety of forms.

In the twentieth century the Irish language continued to play a significant role in Irish community life in Australia among language revivalists and enthusiasts. The language was also a focus for Irish Australians who had an interest in Irish politics. The issues of Home Rule, the Easter Rising of 1916, the Irish Civil War and Irish Independence were reported in Irish Australian newspapers. In turn these issues became a catalyst in the fostering of the Irish language in Australia through language classes. It must also be remembered, however, that native speakers continued to emigrate to Australia throughout the twentieth century. Some of these became involved in the fostering of the language along with Australian-born language enthusiasts. It is likely that there is an even greater interest in and use of the Irish language in Australia today than there has ever been. There are Irish language classes and discussion groups in most capital cities and there are summer and winter intensive language schools in New South Wales and Victoria.

Without Ireland and Irish culture the Irish in Australia have no past. The Irish language alone provides an unbroken connection to Irish Australia's historical self. It is a portable and malleable cultural icon. Whether or not it is used as a means of daily discourse the language in its entirety lies behind each word that appears in print. The Irish language has also been a rich source for Australian expression because wherever there was something new or remarkable an Irish word could be found to express it. The Irish speakers in the nineteenth century in particular travelled to the goldfields and into the Australian interior in search of fortune and adventure. With their free-wheeling English and their native tongue they peppered Australian English with new words when new words were needed. Indeed, some of the most recognised Australian words are in fact Irish words in disguise.

Notes

1 'Queensland for Ever, augus un Ballybug go Braugh', in *Oceans of Consolation*, David Fitzpatrick, Melbourne: Melbourne University Press, 1995, pp. 139–158

2 *Tuam Herald* (Galway) 22 June 1844

3 Archives Office of Tasmania, Hobart (con33/60)

4 Russell Ward, *The Australian Legend,* Melbourne: Oxford University Press, 1971, p. 71

5 Daniel Corkey, *The Hidden Ireland,* Dublin: M.H. Gill and Son, 1941, p. 7

6 *Canberra Sunday Times* (Canberra) 23 January 2000, p. 19

7 Con Costello, *Botany Bay,* Cork: Mercier Press, 1987, p. 87

8 Joseph Holt, *Life of General Joseph Holt*, Sydney: Mitchell Library CY 17.A2024, 1827

9 N. Coughlin. 'The Coming of the Irish to Victoria' in *Historical Studies,* Vol. 12 no. 45, October 1965, 80-81

10 *Freeman's Journal* (Sydney) 28 May 1859

Chapter Two

The Irish Language and Australian English

Crack on to a Sheila

If you don't look for Celtic influences, no-one should be surprised that few Celtic influences have been found.

LORETO TODD[1]

Nobody is quite sure where the English pronoun *she* comes from. It appears in print for the first time in the twelfth century, but before that, the word for the female personal pronoun was *heo*. The Irish language has the female personal pronoun, *sí*, which has the same meaning and the same pronunciation as *she*, but in linguistic circles this Irish connection is not acknowledged. According to Irish academic Loreto Todd, the problem in identifying words originating in any of the Celtic languages is the lack of clear evidence. If compilers of dictionaries are unsure of a word's origins they look to the first written source for a clue. Todd sees this as disadvantaging the recognition of Celtic words because they may not have been written down at the time they first came into English, but she also suggests that an unwritten bias against minority languages is the main problem. In a similar way, David Cairns and Shaun Richards[2] have pointed to the language implications in Shakespeare's *Henry V*, Act 111 Scene 2 where the Welsh, Scots and Irish chiefs are shown speaking their own particular English dialect. For example, the Irish Captain Macmorris uses *ish* for 'is', *tish* for 'it is' and *Chris* for 'Christ'.[3] Cairns and Richards claim that the deviation from standard English by the chiefs is designed to demonstrate the subordinate status of Scotland, Wales and Ireland in the United Kingdom:

> What cannot be acknowledged is their possession of an alternative language and culture, as this would bring into question 'the ideal of a unified English nation'.[4]

If we all speak the same then we are all the same and if we speak differently we are different, at least in theory. Whether the difference is a good or a bad thing seems to depend on how we value this difference in speech. Perhaps we think a language is important because many people speak it: but this is not necessarily the case with Chinese or Spanish. Perhaps we value a language according to how we value the speakers of that language. The French language in itself has no superiority over Spanish or Chinese, and certainly no numerical superiority. However, French, like English is often chosen as an official language in political circles when a choice is required. Celtic languages are clearly not in the same category as the English and French languages. Consequently a judgement placing Celtic languages lower on the list of languages of global importance is not unreasonable.

The issue is of whether Celtic has any value in global terms is not as important as the failure to give it due recognition in the development of the English language. This failure may have come about because of a prejudice against minority languages and in favour of languages of historical importance where etymology is concerned. What is historical importance? Languages may be valued because the society in which they flourished is valued because they attained a high level of civilisation; Greek and Roman society are examples of this. We use the term 'classical' for languages such as Greek and Latin and their literatures because the word 'classical' implies tradition and wide acceptability.

Dictionary-makers follow a particular format in establishing the etymology of a word, and often the first point of reference will be an older dictionary. Dictionaries in other languages may be consulted as well as attention paid to the environment, social, political and geographical situation at the time a word was first captured in print. Great care is taken not to jump to implausible conclusions. Two examples from the *Oxford English Dictionary* serve to demonstrate this. My suggestion that the Irish word *cochall* – 'membrane of the heart' – may be the origin for the phrase 'cockles of the heart', and for which the *OED* had advanced a proposal that the origin lies in the heart being shaped like a cockle, elicited the following reply:

> It does indeed sound a more plausible origin for the phrase than anything mentioned in the *Oxford English Dictionary*. Our first example is from J. Eachard 'Some observations upon the Answer to an enquiry into the grounds & occasions of the contempt of the clergy' (1671) ... Irish etymology had not been considered as a possible origin because there was no evidence that Eachard had any connection with Ireland. Recently, however, some Irish connection has been found and the *OED* will now attribute Irish language origin to the phrase 'cockles of the heart.'[5]

This is an interesting insight into *OED* practice which shows the impor-

THE

IRISH EXILE:

AND FREEDOM'S ADVOCATE.

PUBLISHED EVERY SATURDAY MORNING, AT SEVEN O'CLOCK, PRICE SIX SHILLINGS AND SIX-PENCE PER QUARTER.

No. XLI.—Vol. 1.] HOBART TOWN, SATURDAY, NOVEMBER 2ND, 1850. [Price Six-pence.

CHRISTY'S HATS,

Ex "Derwent,"

Opening ex 'Derwent,' an immense assortment of
GENTLEMEN'S HATS AND CAPS.
Boys & Children's Caps in cloth or velvet
Ladies' Riding Hats (Newest Shape.)
All of which, being bought for Cash, shall be sold at the Lowest remunerating profit

I. G. Reeves.

Exchange Hat Warehouse, Elizabeth-street,
September 20, 1850.

Grindery and Shoemakers' Materials.

Ex "Derwent."

Opening "ex Derwent," 22 Casks and 1 Case Grindery and shoemakers' materials.

These Goods comprise a first-rate assortment, and being purchased for Cash, will be found of excellent value. From the first-rate condition the "Derwent" is turning out her Goods, every article will be warranted sound.

I. G. Reeves.

Exchange Leather Warehouse, Elizabeth-street.

SADDLERS' IRONMONGERY,

Ex "Derwent."

Opening at the Exchange Leather Warehouse,
Ex "DERWENT,"
5 CASES SADDLERS' IRONMONGERY
From the celebrated house of Eldrid, Graves & Co.

These Goods will be found superior to anything heretofore imported to this colony.

CONSISTING OF

Chariot harness mountings
Stage Coach and Gig ditto, in brass and silver
Patent leather collars
Chariot and gig pads furnished
Saddle trees
Polished cart hames
Stirrup irons and bits
Plated spurs
Hunting whips
Patent leather
Buckles in variety

I. G. Reeves.

September, 20th.

WHISKEY! WHISKEY! WHISKEY!

THE undersigned begs to acquaint his friends and the public, that he is enabled to supply them with the best
CAMPBELL TOWN WHISKEY
ever imported to the colony, per *Marmion*

ALSO

Ind and Cope's Ale, in hogsheads
Geneva
Booth's London Gin
Taylor's Porter, Rum, Brandy, &c.

All imported to his order, and selected by a Competent Agent.

Charles Cox.
Salutation Inn, Liverpool-street.

BELL HANGING.

JOHN ANDREW, in returning his sincere thanks for the liberal support he has received from his friends and the public generally for the last 17 years,

To Invalids and Others.

AN Invalid or gentleman requiring country retirement, can be accommodated with Board, and Lodging, and attendance, at a Cottage beautifully situated upon the banks of the Derwent, in the healthy and salubrious district of New Norfolk, within twenty minutes walk of the township. Enquire at the office of this paper, &c., &c., &c.

The "Irish Exile."

IS PUBLISHED EVERY SATURDAY MORNING at 7 o'clock, and circulated throughout the town. An Edition is also forwarded to the country on Friday evening. Persons in the country desirous of becoming subscribers to *The Exile*, are requested to forward their names to the Office, 24 Collins-st., Hobart Town.

"The Irish Exile and Freedom's Advocate" will contain Original Arti-

DILIGENCE COACHES.

BENJAMIN HYRONS,

HAS THE GREATEST PLEASURE and satisfaction in announcing to the public, that he has completed his arrangements for STARTING FOUR HORSE COACHES between HOBART TOWN & LAUNCESTON; & they will commence running on the 1st October, from which period they will run daily, Sundays excepted.

His COACHES ENTIRELY NEW, are perhaps the most elegant and comfortable that ever ran between the two principal towns; and his horses, to procure which he has spared neither expense nor trouble in selection, will be found well broken and quiet.

Altogether he flatters himself that travelling in the DILIGENCE coach, will be experienced more like a Gentleman's Chariot than the coaches commonly employed.

To prevent racing with other coaches that may be on the road, a practice so obnoxious to the traveller, a time bill will be kept and regularly maintained in every stage of the journey; at the same time the greatest expedition will be employed.

Experienced and civil coachmen and guards have been already engaged.

Fares— Inside, £1 10s.; Outside, 15s.

Fourteen pounds of luggage allowed to each passenger, above that a charge will be made. To start from the *Cornwell Hotel*, Launceston, and *Derwent Hotel* Murray-street, Hobart Town, at 6 a.m., the journey to be completed at 7 p.m.

Booking Offices.—In Launceston, at the house lately occupied by Messrs. Francis and Pyle in Charles-street, nearly opposite the establishment of Messrs. Moss & Nathan, and at Hobart Town, the *Derwent Hotel* Murray-street.

N.B.—A branch coach will meet the DILIGENCE from Hobart Town, every evening at Perth, so than passengers and parcels for LONGFORD can be delivered the same evening.

September, 16.

NOTICE! NOTICE!! NOTICE!!

REMOVAL OF
JOHN PERRY,
PLASTERER, PAINTER,
GRAINER, & PAPERHANGER,

WHO returns his sincere and grateful thanks to the Ladies and Gentlemen of Hobart Town and its vicinity, for the liberal support which they have favoured him with for these last four years and begs to acquaint them, that he has taken those Premises now in erection, two doors from Mr. Moir's, Furnishing Ironmonger, Murray-street, for the purpose of more conveniently carrying on his increasing general Business, which he

HAS NOW OPENED

with a new and splendid assortment of Room Papers of the latest arrivals.

☞ Painting, Graining, and the Trade in General, done in town or country, on the most liberal terms.

To the lovers of Harmony

A FREE CONCERT
EVERY EVENING,
AT THE "CITY HOTEL,"
ELIZABETH STREET.
Several Professionals of well-known celebrity are engaged.

Evening Tuition.

NO. 11, MACQUARIE-STREET.

COURSE of INSTRUCTIONS:—A plain English education, together with Mensuration, Practical Geometry

EDUCATION.

T. J. FITZGERALD,

BEGS leave to intimate to the inhabitants of Hobarton, that he has taken a spacious and commodious room in

11, MACQUARIE STREET,

Where he intends to give instructions in a general course of

Classical & Mathematical Literature.

T.J.F. begs leave to assure the Parents and Guardians of Children, that the strictest attention will be paid to the promotion of the literary interests of the pupils who may be entrusted to his care.

The most satisfactory and flattering testimonials can be produced as to competency.

His mode of instructions generally, he presumes, has, for a period of Seven Years in this Colony, met with the unqualified approval of gentlemen of the most distinguished literary acquirements.

Classes will be formed, as soon as practicable, in the following branches, viz.—

Greek—Latin—French—Mathematics Astronomy—Natural Philosophy—History, Sacred and Profane—Geography, Ancient and Modern—Rollin's celebrated system of Belles Lettres and in Drawing.

Lectures will be delivered to the pupils once a month, to which Parents and Guardians are respectfully invited.—Subject of the first Lecture,—

Education as it is at present in Van Diemen's Land.

In conclusion, T.J.F. begs to say, that he has been educated in St. Jarlath's College, under the illustrious Dr. Mac-

The Irish Exile, *published in Hobart 1850–1851. Edited by young Irelander John O'Donohue, a ticket-of-leave convict.*

tance of having evidence of a connection between the first entry of a word and its proposed origins. We may ask, however, assuming that the social and political situation surrounding the first entry for 'cockles of the heart' in 1671 was taken into account, how was the Irish connection missed? Another example is in the word *spree*. Irish has *spraoi*, meaning 'fun, sport, a drinking bout', but the *OED* is hesitant to acknowledge this word as the origin of *spree* (*spraoi* is also pronounced 'spree'). The word *spree* remains as 'origin unknown' in the *Oxford English Dictionary* because the earliest evidence of the word is from the beginning of the nineteenth century and it is found chiefly in Scottish sources. The *OED* would like to have some evidence for how the word came into Scots before they will acknowledge its Irish origin.

It is unlikely that the etymologists at the *OED* are unaware of the movement of Irish people to Britain in the nineteenth century, and that many of these would have been Irish speakers. While there is written evidence to support this in numerous history books, there is little evidence of Irish language writing of the time. Irish was a spoken language, and although there had been books in print in Irish from 1567 they were chiefly religious and scholarly works. It was not until 1882 with the formation of The Gaelic Union that an attempt was made to capture the people's language in print. The first comprehensive Irish English Dictionary, Father Dinneen's *Foclóir Gaedilge*, was not in print until 1904. These are the circumstances that make claims of Celtic or Irish etymology difficult to establish.

The discussion of possible Irish language etymology is not confined to the world of lexicographers. In a discussion in *The Irish Times* in 1999 Deasún Breatnach notes that Diarmaid Ó Muirithe's *A Dictionary of Anglo-Irish* claims that the Old Irish word *peta*, a tame or domesticated animal, is the origin of the English word *pet*. Breatnach finds this supported in Dineen's Irish language dictionary. He finds, however, that this evidence is not supported in *Chambers* (English) *Dictionary*, where, it appears, that 'the Celtic origin is denied emphatically with no authority quoted'.[6]

Encouragingly, awareness of possible Irish language influence on English is growing. For example, *The Australian Oxford Dictionary* (2000) includes a range of Irish language words (such as *gob*, *leprechaun*, *poteen*, *rapparee*, *Sassenach*, *shillelagh* and *spalpeen*) that were not included in the *Australian National Dictionary* (1988). The *AOD* (2000) has also included Irish as a likely origin of the Australian word *kip* as an addition to the traditional 'English dialect' origin proposal. Today there is greater recognition that when Irish people moved in large numbers throughout the world in the nineteenth century they carried the Irish language with them. Words from this language were a natural resource for the naming of new ideas and new items.

The English language was not heard on the continent of Australia before 1788. Unlike most other dialects of English, Australian English can be traced to its beginnings, and we can see clearly how the language began to develop according to this or that influence. English speakers who came to Australia experienced many new things for which they had no words, or for which existing words were not suitable, and so English in Australia began to take on unique characteristics. Another influential factor was the type of English used by the early convicts and settlers. When we think of the convict population and how it outnumbered that of the authorities, we can imagine that lower class English might have flourished in the general English of Australia in a way that would have been unthinkable in Britain. Traditionally people aspiring to speak correctly will copy the speech of the dominant class. However, in early European Australia there was such an imbalance in the population that the dominant influence was the lower classes, and this accounts for many characteristics of Australian English, especially slang.

The development of European Australia, as an after-thought of the Penal Colony, meant that the upper classes or aristocracy were not represented in colonial Australia. Early Colonial Australia was overwhelmingly lower-class and there was a disproportionate number of speakers of English regional dialects. The result was that the traditional balance of power between upper class British English and those dialects shifted in Australia. People may also aspire to using the type of English they read in good literature and we may presume that among the convict population access to literary works would have been limited. Without a literary standard it is difficult to set a standard for correct English. There is no body to condemn the use of slang or to correct bad English and so anything can be acceptable.

Australia's distinctive English vocabulary also includes words from indigenous Australian languages, such as the names for landscape items, flora and fauna, and weapons, as well as customs and traditions that were new to the colonisers. New words also came from American English as Americans and Australians mingled in the search for gold, first in California in 1849 and later in Australia. It was during this time that the Australian term *shouting*, as in paying for a round of drinks, became part of Australian English. The Irish were the ones to bring this term, however, from the word *glaoigh* meaning to call or to shout and the phrase *glaoch ar dheoch* meaning to call or shout for drink. Irish speakers in translating from Irish to English picked the word 'shout' as a translation for *glaoch*. Perhaps the term to shout for a drink passed into the general population because it suited the crowded and noisy atmosphere of a goldfield's 'bar' where you had to shout for your drink in order to be heard.

While translating from Irish to English was one way the Irish brought new words into Australian English, the other way was in their use of a dialect of English that was not standard English but which was the only English the Irish knew. Speakers of other English dialects would have been aware of the mainstream vocabulary even if they chose not to use it. For example, today most Australians would know that the slang word *dunny* has its mainstream equivalent in the word *toilet* and would not use the term *dunny* in certain circles. Someone whose first language is not English might not learn to make that distinction. Another thing we can observe in Australian English is that words such as *dale, glen, meadow, valley* and *wood* are not used, except in place names. Perhaps the Australian landscape was so different to early settlers that these words simply did not fit, but it is more likely that these were literary words and that the majority of the population, including the Irish, would not have been familiar with them. The Irish were a large enough group who spoke non-standard English (without being aware of it) to have influenced the development of non-standard English in Australia. The Irish were possibly like the Americans where the English language is concerned: they were unconstrained by convention and had their own English dialect which was an acceptable standard. They also had the whole vocabulary of the Irish language to draw on when a word was needed for a new situation.

Irish Words in Australian English

Language is worth studying because, David Crystal says, it can give us clues to how people lived and about their cultural contacts.[7] We can see this in Irishman William Kelly's account of his experience working in a Victorian goldmine in 1859:

> When I attained the surface I procured some water to wash in, for my head, face, beard, and hand were coated with clauber, made up of dirt and perspiration.[8]

Kelly provides a footnote for the word *clauber* which he says is 'a sort of consistent paste made of mud and moisture, unknown to Johnson'. The 'Johnson' referred to is undoubtedly Samuel Johnson, England's famous eighteenth-century lexicographer.

The word clauber is most certainly Irish *clábar*, the word for 'mud', and despite Kelly being an Irishman, and from a part of the country where he would have been exposed to Irish, his reference to Samuel Johnson shows the educated mindset of the time which looks to England for origins, and with good reason. William Kelly's family owned a large flax dyeing factory in Sligo. Like many of his class, he was probably educated in England. He became a magistrate in Sligo before he took up the life of a traveller and observer in the colonies. Kelly's comment tells us that he has an interest in unusual words and that his presumption is that *clauber* is an unknown English word. Had Samuel Johnson been familiar with the word *clauber* it is unlikely that he would have included it in his dictionary as in English it would have been a slang word. In the Irish language, however, *clábar* is a standard word and so would have been used readily by Irish-speakers in the muddy conditions of the Australian goldfields. For newcomers to the goldfields, such as Kelly, the word *clábar* would have assisted in breaking down communication barriers on the goldfields, all sharing at least this one word. We get a sense in Kelly's description that, while the word was new for him, it had become a universally accepted word to describe the dirty condition of both body and clothing after a day fossicking or gold digging.

There are only three known occurrences of this word *clauber* in Australian literature. The next occurrence of the word after its use by William Kelly is in Henry Handel Richardson's *The Fortunes of Richard Mahony* where it again refers to the mud and dirt that clings to the skin after a day at the 'diggings'. The third occurrence is in Lesley Haylen's *Big Red* (1965) where, if the same word is in question, there has been a shift in meaning: 'I don't want to shovel up great clabbers of horse dung in the mornin''. This would appear to be a reference to manure in a wet state and perhaps in the Irish Australian setting the Irish word *clábar* became applied to a similar substance when the English word was not known. The suitability of the word for Irish conditions is evident in its retention in the English of Ireland. Diarmaid Ó Muirithe in his *A Dictionary of Anglo-Irish* includes the word *clábar*, anglicised as *clabber* and *clauber*. One of Ó Muirithe's citations is a line from one of Seamus Heaney's poems: 'Or in the sucking clabber I would splash'. The word *clábar* may also have been retained because mud was a common building material in Ireland.

While the goldfield use of the word *clábar* was short-lived, it may be that the word also formed the basis of the word *clobber*, 'old clothes'. The first *OED* entry for *clobber* meaning 'old clothes', is from 1879. We have seen the possibility for Irish *clábar* 'mud' being used in a new setting, the goldfields. Could the word have been transferred to describe the clothes the miners would have worn? It is unlikely that this clothing would have been washed every day, and so would have been constantly covered in *clábar*. It is a short step then to imagine a generic description of such clothes as *clobber*, and in turn that the word would be applied to old clothes in general.

Irish language influence is most apparent in Australian slang. As Irish was initially a prohibited language in Australia, and as the Irish, in general, occupied the lower rungs of early European Australian society, this is not surprising. The first written account of slang words in Australia is James Hardy Vaux's collection of convict terminology as presented to the Governor in 1812. In that collection are a number of terms of probable Irish origin; for example, *fawney* 'a finger-ring' from Irish *fáinne* 'a ring' and the term *tinny* 'a fire' from Irish *tine* 'a fire'. In addition the term 'out-and-out' meaning 'completely' is similar to Irish *amach is amach* 'completely', but literally 'out and out'. The term 'screeve' meaning 'a letter' may be from Latin or one of the Romance languages, but Irish also has Latin based *scríobh* pronounced 'screeve' and meaning 'to write'.

Between 1900 and 1910 S.E. O'Brien and A.G. Stephens collected a range of Australian words, some of which may also point to Irish language influence. For example, the word *balter*, the collectors claim, is Anglo-Irish and signifies 'on the street'. The Irish word for 'street' is *bóther*, pronounced 'boe-her' but which has had other pronunciations such as in the Dublin suburb Stoneybatter. Diarmaid Ó Muirithe records the forms of *batter*, *boker*, *bater*, and *boagher*, but not O'Brien and Stephen's *bolher*. The term *bolher* appears to be an isolated find in the O'Brien and Stephens' collection, as I have not seen it in any other dictionaries or word lists. It is interesting, however, that O'Brien and Stephens discuss the word as if it were relatively common (in the world of slang). Is this the Irish word for 'road' that has undergone a change in Australia? The word is also similar to the Australian word *battler*, historically a word with a range of meanings, from the current term for a hard worker from humble origins to the older meaning of someone who is unemployed, and before that to an itinerant worker, and ultimately it was a word for a prostitute. The origin of the word is supposed to be English *battle,* which seems to me unlikely. As all of the early meanings of the word *battler* can be connected with being on the street or on the road, it may be that Irish *bóthar* 'street/road' and Anglo-Irish *bolher* lie somewhere behind this Australian word.

Related to the *battler* is the *bludger*. This word and those that follow in this discussion were suggested to me by native Irish speakers in Australia as having parallels in Irish. *The Australian National Dictionary* suggests that the word *bludger* is a survival of British slang, where *bludger* is a shortened form of *bludgeoner*, someone who bludgeons. The first citing is from 1895; the word *bludger* being the word for a pimp. The modern interpretation of the word, the generalised term of abuse for someone who lives off other people's efforts, for example a dole bludger, is first recorded in 1900. Irish has the word *bleidire*, 'a wheedler' or an 'impertinent fellow or a flatterer'. It sounds like 'bledgerer'. The word *bludger(er)*, may come from Irish, because its sense suits the idea of a pimp who wheedles and cajoles others to earn a living for him (or to use his services). Someone who does this could be seen to be lazy: the modern interpretation of *bludger*. Irish *bleidire* seems a more satisfying source for *bludger* than a word that signifies a violent act.

Another Australian slang term worth looking at in this search for Irish language origins is *cack*, 'to void excrement'. This word is certainly found in English dialects but the last citation in the *OED* is 1731. The word *cack* is also a common European word, having parallels in Latin, Middle Dutch, Dutch, Polish and Early Modern German. Irish has *cac* as the standard Irish language word for 'voiding excrement'. In Dublin, which has been English-speaking for hundreds of years, the word *caca* remains the word children are taught for excrement in the same way that *poo* is used elsewhere. Although the word as it occurs in Australian English may have come from any of the European languages listed above, the presence of large numbers of Irish in Australia points to the likelihood that Irish *cac* lies behind the slang word *cack* that is heard in a phrase such as 'I cacked my pants'.

In the same way, the Australian word *chook*, meaning 'chicken' or 'hen' may have become popular because even in English-speaking rural Irish this is the sound made to call hens and chickens to feed. In this case the word is Irish *tioc*, the imperative of the verb 'to come'. We may expect a word associated with an essential occupation to be retained under a language shift, so we can imagine that Irish migrants to Australia with a rural background would continue to use the word *tioc* to call the fowl. *Tioc* is pronounced 'chook'. Diarmaid Ó Muirithe records it in the form *tiuc* and *tiuci*. The word *tioc*, then, is prevalent not only in Irish language speech but also in Irish English. The first Australian citing of *chook* is 1855, a time when Irish migrant figures were peaking. By contrast, the *Oxford English Dictionary*'s first citation for 'chuck' (the sound made by a hen) is 1386, and while the last entry is 1860 the word *chuck* in this citation refers to a sound used to call horses. If the British dialect word for calling hens was no longer current in the middle of the nineteenth century, it may be that in nineteenth century Australia Irish *tioc* was either a reinforcer of a sound already in British dialect, or the origin of the Australian word *chook*.

The Australian phrase 'to crack on to someone', meaning to chat someone up for the purpose of having sexual relations, is well known Australian slang. While it is usually attributed to some variation in the use of the word *crack*, the sexual connotations of the phrase to crack on to someone resonates with Irish language speakers in Australia because it resembles the Irish language word *craiceann* which means 'skin', but which is also a word in the term for 'sexual intercourse': *bualadh craiceann*, sexual intercourse, is literally 'beating skin'. In Irish *bean chraicinn* is the word for a 'prostitute' (*bean* = woman). If

Australian *crack on* is really *craiceann* in disguise, we can be sure that it originated from native Irish language speakers who had a word to share that was known to them but which was a secret word that could be used openly. In the absence of any other explanation for the Australian slang phrase *crack on to someone*, the Irish connection is worth mentioning.

This has been a necessarily brief study of possible Irish influence on Australian slang. Some proposals carry more weight than others, but I suggest that all should be examined and that further research in this area will yield more fruit. Slang by its nature is difficult to track. By the time slang words appear in print they may have undergone many changes, making the origins of these words difficult to determine with any certainty. To compound matters, time and distance have masked the Irish language connection with Australia. By contrast, standard Australian English has a more stable and long term history in print, and here we can also find Irish language words at work in naming new experiences and new items.

The language of the eighteenth- and nineteenth-century Irish in Australia was a repository of their values and beliefs. Their world view was Catholic, conservative and rural, and in Australia they would experience not only a new landscape and climate but also different value systems. For some this experience began on the voyage out. These factors must be considered when considering Irish origins for Australian words, and they were certainly influential in the birth of that iconic Australian word *sheila.*

The strength of the *Oxford English Dictionary*'s etymological aspect is its emphasis on historical principles. In theory the first recorded example of a word should provide clues as to its origin. Of course when this does not eventuate, or when the wrong conclusion is drawn, the result can be self-perpetuating, most dictionaries tending to follow those that precede. A new edition of a dictionary tends to focus on new additions and rarely makes changes to existing entries. This is borne out by the history of the recorded etymology of the Australian word *sheila.* In 1828 the Sydney newspaper *The Monitor* reported a street fight which occurred on Saint Patrick's Day. The report included the comment that following the fight 'many a piteous Shela stood wiping the gory locks of her Paddy'.[9] The *OED* (1989) defines the word *sheila* as:

> a young girl or young woman; a girlfriend. Playfully affectionate and predominantly in male use.

The *OED* also includes the Irish origin of the word:

> It may represent a generic use of the (originally Irish) personal name *Sheila*, the counterpart of *Paddy* ... in any case, it became assimilated to this at some later stage.

and also mentions an earlier English dialect word *shaler*. We can detect some uncertainty in the *OED* commentary on the word *sheila*; a sense that some information does not fit, something is missing. On the other hand, there is no such hesitation in the entry of *sheila* in *The Dinkum Dictionary* (2003).

> 'Sheila' was a common female name in Ireland, used alongside the name 'Paddy' to represent the archetypal Irish couple. From this early usage (dating from the 1820s in Britain) 'Sheila' came to mean any female, whether Irish or not. This British use of 'sheila' was then transported to the colonies.[10]

I suggest that the reason lexicography has had difficulty explaining the origins of the Australian English word *sheila* is because of an error made from the beginning. It is surprising that no one, apparently, has questioned these written assertions that the name *Sheila* is common in Ireland. It is not. Nor has the name *Sheila* ever been used in the generic sense of a counterpart to *Paddy* in Ireland. Neither was the name *Sheila* common in eighteenth or nineteenth century Ireland. Between 1788 and 1828 over two thousand female convicts were transported to Australia from Irish ports. The most common name was Mary, followed by Ann/e, Catherine, Margaret, Elizabeth, Brigid and Sara. These, of course, are official first names. Many of these women would have used Irish names or diminutives of the English names, such as: *Máire, Áine, Cáit, Kitty, Kathleen, Peg, Maggie, Éilis, Bríd, Bridie* and *Biddy*. There were no Sheilas on board these convict ships. The Irish name *Síle* is rendered in English as *Julia*, but there were no *Julia*s on board either. That the word *sheila* is a term for a woman or girl in Australia is indisputable, but in Ireland this is not the case. The name *Biddy*, a shortened form of *Brigid*, is the only likely counterpart to the generic *Paddy*, and this name was used in America in the nineteenth century for a domestic servant.

So where did Australian *sheila* come from? I suggest that the answer lies in Irish English *sheela* or *sheelah*, meaning an effeminate male, one who spends too much time in women's company. This Irish English word in turn comes from the Irish language word *Síle*, 'homosexual'. G.A. Wilkes in his discussion of *sheila* states that 'no woman would refer to herself as a "sheila" '.[11] The use of the term *sheila* by males towards males in Australia has been officially recognised, albeit only recently. *The Penguin Book of Australian Slang* records a secondary meaning for *sheila* as: 'A man who is weak, effeminate, lacking in bravado'.[12] Here, I suggest, is a connection with the definitions discussed earlier of the Irish word *Síle* and Irish English sheela(h). It is significant that in Australia the official recognition that *sheila* may be used by males of males arises in a dictionary of slang because it is likely that Australian *sheila* was at one time a slang or even taboo word. In Ireland, the only dictionary to admit to the meaning of 'homosexual' for the word *Síle* is

Foclóir na Collaíochta, Dáithí Ó Luineacháin's dictionary of sexual terminology, which is written entirely in the Irish language. The information in this dictionary is not for general consumption.

Hugh Brody outlines a divide in the roles of a typical rural Irish husband and his wife in the 1970s in his anthropological study of family and community in the West of Ireland.[13] The daily ritual consisted of the wife rising first and preparing breakfast for her husband and the children. The husband then went to work in the fields. The couple never ate together, and in the evenings it was customary for the husband to visit neighbours or have neighbours visit him while his wife continued with the household and family work. Finally the husband went to bed before his wife. Male and female lived separate lives, in effect, due to 'a highly developed division of sexual roles'. We can presume that any noticeable crossing of this divide would have been commented upon, and in the case of a male, through the use of terminology such as *Síle* (along with other Irish language words that indicate effeminacy, such as *cistineoir* and *piteog*).

Those eighteenth- and nineteenth-century Irish convicts who were transported to Australia would have experienced not only a change in landscape and climate but also a way of life that was new and no doubt alienating. Especially in those early days when there was a shortage of females, and considering what might have been required of a convict serving in a penal colony, work such as washing clothes, cooking and cleaning would have fallen to the male. It may be that those who were seen to be doing this work well, or who may have taken undue interest in it, would have been ridiculed for demonstrating effeminacy. In this climate males may well have applied the term *Síle* to such males. However, given the double use of the word *Síle* in Ireland, to denote not just effeminacy but also homosexuality, we must conclude that the surfacing of this Irish word in Australia may have been prompted by stress, when Irish convicts witnessed homosexuality.

Many Irish convicts transported to Australia were from rural areas, brought up with social norms peculiar to their own small world. Even before arrival in Australia, conditions on board the convict ships would have necessitated participation in what may have been considered women's work: cooking, cleaning, the washing of clothes and so on. Homosexual activity was common on board the convict ships and later in Australia. In Hyde Park barracks in Sydney, young boys especially were preyed upon by old lags. One naïve, but probably typical, Irish youth complained to the Catholic bishop at the time that there was no such activity (meaning homosexual activity) in Ireland.[14] An 1847 report on Norfolk Island noted that while English convicts turned to sodomy the Irish Catholics did not.[15] The Irish-speaking convicts had a word for a person who took part in homosexual activity; he was a *Síle*. This word was known and understood among the Irish convicts and could be passed on to others, but yet was a secret word and safe to use even in the hearing of authorities. The circumstances favourable to the continued use of the Irish language word *Síle* in Australia were: the reversal of male/female domestic roles; homosexual activity of a violent nature; and strong religious beliefs.

The probability that Irish *Síle* meaning 'homosexual' is the origin for Australian *sheila* is further enhanced when we consider that the word *sheila* as a generic name for an (Irish) female did not surface in Britain or in America, countries which experienced far greater numbers of Irish settlers than did Australia. The Australian word *sheila* is geographical. It reflects the nature of Australian society at that time. Finally, the Australian word *sheila* is a word used almost exclusively by males, is always slightly derogatory when used of females, and, according to *The Penguin Book of Australian Slang*, can also mean 'a man who is weak, effeminate, lacking in bravado'. In the underworld where slang lives, this connotation for Australian *sheila* more clearly reflects an origin in Irish *Síle*, 'effeminate male', 'homosexual,' than the traditionally held origin of the Irish Christian name *Sheila*.[16]

Another area that may yield Irish lexicographical fruit is Aboriginal Englishes and Australian languages. Jakelin Troy in her study of New South Wales Pidgin notes that the Irish language word *pampúta* can be found in the vocabulary of the Aborigines of western New South Wales for the word 'shoe'.[17] This is supported by Tamsin Donaldson whose *Macquarie Aboriginal Words* cites the word *pampuu* as Ngiyampa for 'shoe'.[18] The Irish usage is largely confined to the Aran islands off the west coast of Ireland, the shoes being made from rawhide. The *pampooties*, as they are known in Irish English, were worn as far back as 700 AD. The survival of this word in an Aboriginal language may be due to intense and prolonged contact with Irish speakers from the Aran islands, or simply because the Irish provided a word to this Aboriginal tribe for a new item, footwear.

Along with *Síle* and *pampúta* we can consider the Irish word *cipín* ('small stick or twig'), accredited by the *Australian Oxford Dictionary* (2000) as a probable origin for the word *kip*, the name for the piece of word used in the game 'two-up' (the ending *ín* in *cipín* is a diminutive). Here is another example where the Irish had a word to offer for something new in Australia; namely the flat stick used in two-up for tossing coins. It is likely that the first *kip* was a piece of stick or wood found lying about and called simply that by Irish speakers. From there it became a special word to be used in the context of a two-up game. Over time the Irish origin was forgotten, if indeed it was ever widely known. Certainly any connection between the Australian word *kip* and an Irish language word would have been lost as the numbers of Irish speakers diminished with the drop in Irish immigration in the twentieth century.

The word *spree* as used in Australia is another word with a likely Irish language origin that has been transformed under new conditions. *Spree* is from Irish *spraoi* meaning 'fun, 'sport', or as a secondary meaning, 'a prolonged drinking bout' and it is the latter use that has flourished in Australia and America. In a previous study[19] of Irish language words occurring in Anglo-Irish writing over two hundred years, I found only one reference to the secondary meaning for *spraoi*. This would appear to indicate that the social conditions that would produce the long drinking bout were not frequent (at least not frequent enough to be recorded) in Ireland. In Australian writing, however, the word *spree,* a favourite word of many authors, and its meaning in terms of a wild outburst of behaviour, usually accompanied by alcohol, is close to the Irish use of the term. The following collection of occurrences of the word *spree* is from the Glossary at the end of this book:

> **Spraoi** n. in form **spree**. **1**. 'fun', 'sport' **2**. 'a prolonged drinking bout' **1853** Ellen Clancy, *A Lady's Visit to the Gold Diggings of Australia* 66: They were returning to Melbourne for a spree; **1865** Henry Kingsley, *The Hillyars and the Burtons* 203: I was lost in contemplation of such a gigantic spree; **1882** Lucy Sussex, *The Fortunes of Mary Fortune* 77: Such a spree as was that night held around the doctor's insensible body; **1883** Edward M. Curr, *Recollections of Squatting in Victoria* 174: the old convict custom of going to town once a year 'to have a spree'; **1888** Henry Lawson, 'A Wild Irishman' in *Short Stories and Sketches* 190: while he was on 'spree'; **1889** Rolf Boldrewood, *Robbery Under Arms* 79: The other chaps were wild for a spree; **1895** Henry Goldsmith, *Euancondit* 7: 'My mate went off on a spree'; **1898** Edward Dyson, 'The Golden Shanty' in *Below and On Top and Other Stories* 99: to revel in an occasional 'spree'; **1908** E.S. Sorenson, *The Squatter's Ward* 33: 'So we reckoned on havin' a real good spree.'; **1926** Marion Miller Knowles, *Pierce O'Grady's Daughter* 230: 'he's a foul-mouthed brute when on a spree after a pay-out'; **1930** Henry Handel Richardson, *The Fortunes of Richard Mahony* 55: had profited by his absence to empty the cash box and go off on the spree; **1932** Jim McCarthur, *Pan's Clan* 131: 'To me he doesn't look like coming peacefully away for a spree at the present moment'; **1934** Brian Penton, *Landtakers* 210: 'He's out on the spree there this three weeks'; **1946** Katherine Susannah Prichard, *The Roaring Nineties* 65: nothing less than a champagne spree; **1948** Ruth Park, *The Harp in the South* 61: 'She felt sure that Hughie was going on a Christmas spree.'; **1954** 'John O'Brien', 'When the 'Sut' Drops Down' in *The Parish of St Mel's* 48: And Brother Ted came home today to see his folk between the sprees; **1959** Mary Durack, *Kings in Grass Castles* 163: bragging, swaggering, fighting and coming together on lively sprees; **1965** Leslie Haylen, *Big Red* 3: Red's father had been on the spree for days now; **1966** Bill Beatty, *Tales of Old Australia* 97: a desire to

S.T. Gill's sketch shows an Irish immigrant with characteristic Irish dress and the short pipe dúidín, *or 'dudeen'.* NATIONAL LIBRARY OF AUSTRALIA

shake of the effects of a heavy spree; **1997** Ann McGrath 'Sexuality and Australian Identities' in *Creating Australia* 46: White men blew their earnings on a 'gin-spree' or orgy of alcohol and Aboriginal women; **1999** Kim Scott, *Benang* 221: When there was a spree, stay clear away. It was not safe.

We can see that the Irish in Australia had a word to describe a social phenomenon, that of drinking to excess after a long period of abstinence. The word *spree* is a perfect word for the Australian social conditions of the nineteenth century that saw many people isolated from recreational pursuits for long periods of time, whether on the goldfields or squatting on tracts of land or shepherding in the bush. The use of the word in the abuse of indigenous people in the last two quotations suggests a further development in the meaning of this word in Australia.

There are Irish resonances in the Australian word *waddy* which may have influenced its spread throughout Australia. The spelling of the Australian word *waddy* has varied over time from 'wad-di' or 'waddy' to 'woo-da' and then 'whaddie' and 'waddie'. The spelling 'wood-da' suggests a completely different pronunciation than that which we associate with the Australian word *waddy*. The use of the hyphen suggests care taken to separate the syllables in conveying pronunciation. While most of these spellings are of the Australian word that means a fighting stick, the spelling 'whaddie' in 1798 refers to a type of boomerang. It appears from this that there are two words under discussion. In Ireland the Irish language word *maide*, 'a stick', has the anglicised forms 'midyee', 'muddiagh', 'muddie' and 'waddy'. In Irish 'mh' changes to 'w' under lenition (i.e. a change of sound with change in case). Lenition occurs in a range of instances, such as when the possessive pronoun is used, say in, *do mhaide* 'your stick'. This would then be pronounced 'waddja' or 'waddy'.

The *Australian National Dictionary* provides a secondary meaning for the Aboriginal word *waddy*: 'a club or cudgel as used by a person other than an Aboriginal'. I have been informed that the word *waddy* was used in a Christian Brother's school in Sydney in the 1950s. What we may have here is evidence of cross-cultural and linguistic contact in early eighteenth-century European Australia. Irish speakers, hearing a word similar to their own may have given the Aborigines the name for the sticks they carried. In turn the Aborigines, believing it to be an English word, may have learned it. Subsequently, the English speakers who heard the word from the Aborigines may have assumed it was an Aboriginal word. The other possible scenario is that by coincidence both languages had the same sounding word for the same item and that the Irish one took precedence, at least in the extension of meaning to include a weapon used by a non-Aboriginal. This may account for the various spellings of the word and why one version, at least, does not refer to a stick or cudgel. Once again the Irish word may have been the reinforcer in the spread of an Australian word.

Another word that I suggest may have Irish origins is *brumby*. Irish has *bromach* 'a colt' and its plural is *bromaigh*, pronounced 'brummy'. The word is used to describe a strong young man or an awkward young man. As such it is a popular word both in the Irish-speaking communities and outside of them in the English of Ireland. The *Australian National Dictionary* provides *brombie*, *brumbie* and *brummy* as variations of *brumby*. The first dictionary citation is from Queensland and the second from New South Wales, which suggests that the word was in widespread use before it was captured in print. The citations up until 1893 are of the word in plural form. As the Irish plural *bromaigh* is pronounced *brummy* this could have been either the origin of the word or a reinforcer of one of the other supposed avenues of origin, such as people with the surname Brumby. As most discussions cite *brumby* as 'of unknown origin', and theories of the word originating from a surname are tenuous, it makes sense to add the Irish language word *bromaigh* for consideration as a possible source of Australian *brumby*.

The *Australian National Dictionary* records the first dictionary entries for the word *didgeridoo* as 1919, surprisingly late in the history of European Australia. In that year, the *Huon Times* (Franklin) refers to the instrument as a 'Diridgery doo'. The magazine *Smith's Weekly* (Sydney) in the same year cites as the sound of the instrument 'didjerry, didjerry, didjerry'. In 1924 the *Bulletin* (Sydney) provides 'Didjeridoo-didjeredoo!'. In the 1967 entry, F.T.A. MacCartney suggested that the name *didgeridoo* is 'imitative' of the sound of the instrument. MacCartney also suggests that *didgeridoo* is not an Aboriginal word. This view was repeated in 1990 in the discussion of the word in *Australian Aboriginal Words in English*.[20] The didgeridoo instrument is found mainly in the upper half of Australia. As there are many Aboriginal languages in Australia, so there are numerous Aboriginal words for this musical instrument. Some examples are: *bambi, bombo, illpera* and *yidali*. None of these words resembles the word *didgeridoo*.

Even if the word *didgeridoo*, is not from an Australian language, it still sounds 'Australian'. It resembles other familiar Australian names, such as, *cockatoo, jackaroo, kangaroo,* the more recent *socceroo* and place names such as Woolloomooloo. It may, indeed, have been coined under that influence. The claim that the word *didgeridoo* is 'imitative' is a curious one in retrospect. The sound of the word *didgeridoo* hardly represents the repetitive 'drone' or 'hum' that we associate with this instrument. In order to test this theory, I conducted an informal survey where I asked participants to 'write in letters the sound of the didgeridoo'. The results are as follows:

Derrrrr
Mwaaahhh Briheehe Mawawworrr
Mwoooowowoowoopwoopwooooowmmmnoop woooowwoooooow
Blum-to-to-to
Mmmberrrrrrr
wahaaawaa
ooommm
brrrr-ri!
Ngnnn! nya nya
Nynn!

boing
ooowahooyeeoowooo
wurr! wurr! woww!
Doo ooo ooo Dooo oo Doooom ooom Dooo
Brrowwwwwwwhewheerroouw
oo aa oo aa
mmm ...
waaaaaaaaaaaaaaanrm
bwarrararra cucucucubwrww
Baarrooooowooowoooowawooo
mmmwoobwoob woob wah woo woo woo
mmmmmm,
mirbooh
mooonarau
erranamabraera
mmrrrrmmrrrmrrmr
Mowowerrmowromdoodoodoodoowmowerrmrm

Most respondents represented the sound of the *didgeridoo* in a series of letters starting with the letter 'm'. The next popular choice was the letter 'b'. None of the respondents produced letters similar to the word *didgeridoo*. I suggest that those who produced the letters Drrrr and Doo ooo ooo etc. may have been influenced by the word *didgeridoo*. By and large the word *didgeridoo* does not appear to represent the sound of the instrument and so is not 'imitative'. If the word *didgeridoo* is not really imitative of the sound of the instrument and is not a word from an Australian language, where did it come from?

Both Irish and Scots Gaelic have the word *dúdaire* which cognates with the word *dúid*, 'a pipe'. The word *dúdaire* is used in Ireland to mean 'an incessant pipe-smoker' or 'an inquisitive person'. Niall Ó Dónaill's (1977) Irish-English dictionary refers to 'a long-nosed person' and the sound of 'crooning' or 'droning'. Dineen's 1904 Irish-English dictionary provides as translation of *dúdaire* 'a trumpeter or horn-blower, blowing of a horn, act of crooning or humming'. Malcolm Maclennan's *Gaelic Dictionary* (1979) provides the translation 'trumpeter'.[21] The word *dúdaire* is a tri-syllabic word, pronounced, roughly, 'dooderreh', or 'doodjerreh'. Irish and Scots Gaelic also have the words *dubh* 'black', pronounced 'duv' or 'doo' and the word *dúth* 'native or hereditary', also pronounced 'doo'. It is possible that the distinctive Australian sound of *didgeridoo* is, in fact, an Irish one. It may be that Irish or Scots Gaelic speakers gave the name *dúdaire dubh* or *dúdaire dúth* (pronounced 'doodereh doo or 'doojerreh doo') to the person playing the native instrument and that the word became associated with the instrument. This theory would explain the curious incompatibility between the word *didgeridoo* and the sound of the instrument. The Irish may have been more interested in the person who played the instrument than in the instrument itself, perhaps, in admiration for the artistry it takes to produce the didgeridoo sounds.

The Irish brought their native language with them to Australia and used it in everyday life. It was their natural form of greeting and the language that spoke their emotions. The language reflected their culture, values and beliefs. For the Aran islander the word *pampúta* was the word for a shoe. The word *bromach* was a popular term for a young spirited horse for the rural Irish. A *cipín* was another popular word; a generic term for a small piece of wood such as might be found lying around and which could be used as a makeshift item to toss coins. Likewise a *waddy* was an everyday item in those days of faction fighting. The Irish are a strong musical nation whose history extends as far back as the Bronze Age and ancient horns. While the drone of such musical instruments was a familiar sound, the expertise of the Aboriginal player was more worthy of note as we can see in the term *dúdaire dubh*.

The vibrant and talkative Irish spread around the country and their characteristic way of speaking was often recorded. Writers have captured for us the Irish voice in Australia according to what they have heard or read. While the Irish voice in Australian fiction may or may not represent the truth, the words the writer chooses to depict that voice are often words that have travelled in the Irish language for centuries, and arrived in Australia near the end of the twentieth. This is the subject of the next chapter.

Notes

1 Loreto Todd, 'Where Have All the Celtic Words Gone?' in *English Today*, 63, Vol. 16 No. 3 July 2000. 6-9.

2 David Cairns and Shaun Richard, 'What Ish My Nation', in *The Post-Colonial Reader*. 178-180.

3 William Shakespeare, *Henry V*, London: Penguin Books, 1968.

4 Bill Ashcroft, Gareth Griffiths and Helen Tiffin (eds), *The Post-Colonial Studies Reader*, London: Routledge. 1995. 180.

5 Samantha Schad, personal communication, 16 November 2000.

6 *The Irish Times,* 20 April 1999.

7 Paul Lang, *The English Language Debate*, Springfield, N.J.: Enslow Publishers, Inc., 1995. 30

8 William Kelly, *Life in Victoria,* Kylmore, Victoria: Lowden Publishing Co., 1977. 220.

9 *The Monitor* (Sydney) 22 March 1828.

10 Susan Butler, *The Dinkum Dictionary,* Melbourne: Text Publishing, 2001. 164.

11 G.A. Wilkes, *A Dictionary of Australian Colloquialisms*, Oxford: Oxford University Press, 1996. 337.

12 Lenie Johansen, *The Penguin Book of Australian Slang*, Melbourne: Penguin Books, 1996. 363.

13 Hugh Brody, *Inishkillane: Change and Decline in the West of Ireland*, London: Pelican Books, 1974. 112.

14 ibid. 268.

15 Robert Hughes, *The Fatal Shore*, London: William Collins, 1987. 538.

16 This does not mean that there is not a connection between the two words. The Irish form of the English name 'Julia' is *Síle*, pronounced 'Sheila' and is probably derived from Saint Cecilia. Another word *Síle* has a generic sense in the Irish language, for example *Síle na gCíoch*, the name given to grotesque female figures adorning the walls of churches and of an uncertain origin; *Síle na bPíce* 'earwig', literally '*Síle* of the Forks', *Síle na bPortach* 'heron', literally, '*Síle* of the Bog' and in the phrase *Síle chaoch a dhéanamh de dhuine*, literally 'to make a *Síle* of someone', figuratively 'to make a fool of someone'. The histories surrounding these words and phrases have been lost with the loss of the Irish language.

17 Jakelin Troy, 'Der mary this is fine cuntry is there is in the wourld', in *The Irish Immigrant Experience in Australia*, eds John O'Brien and Pauric Travers, Dublin: Poolbeg Press, 1991. 165.

18 *Macquarie Aboriginal Words*, Nick Thieberger and William McGregor eds., Sydney: The Macquarie Library Pty Ltd, 1999. 28.

19 Dymphna Lonergan, 'The Significance of the Irish Language in Anglo-Irish Writing 1800–1989', MA thesis, Flinders University of South Australia, 1994. 18.

20 R.M. Dixon, W.S. Ramson and Mandy Thomas, *Australian Aboriginal Words in English*, Melbourne: Oxford University Press. 1990.

21 Malcolm Maclennan, *Gaelic Dictionary*, Edinburgh: Acair Press. 1979. 138.

chapter three

Writing Irish Australia

Bulls, Blunders and Follies

Irish characters in Australian literature seldom play major roles. As minor players, they are often comic characters that the hero or heroine of a novel encounters along the way. They provide light relief mainly because of the way they speak. Irish English is a non-standard English that reflects the bilingual history of Ireland, such as when an Irish person says *press* for 'cupboard', or 'the likes of'. Overall, Irish English emerged from an Irish language background and this, perhaps, is its most distinctive feature. The Irish dialect of English, then, is of great interest to writers who wish to include Irish characters in their plays or novels. The Australian writer who portrays Irish characters can be assured of a good reception from the many readers of Irish descent. The social history of the Irish in Australia has been significant. Irish Australian ancestral echoes are strong, from the enduring story of Ned Kelly to the Irish influence on Australian politics and working life.

The nineteenth-century Irish moved into English-speaking Britain and Australia in large numbers, and with their Irish language and their strange English, they were noticed and noted. In England the Irish presence was a reminder of the testy political relationship between England and Ireland. In Australia the Irish were loud and complaining under the system of transportation, and unruly and inexpert 'orphan' servants. The Irish character in an Australian novel is not only imitative of real life, but also represents a stock literary character. Consequently, the introduction of an Irish character into an Australian novel is certain to evoke an active response of recognition from the reader. Whether that response is positive or negative depends on how the Irish character is represented and the part he or she plays in the plot.

Irish English

The form of English known as Irish English has its history in the colonisation of Ireland, which ultimately resulted in the loss of the Irish language. The

English language came to Ireland in the twelfth century, and by the fifteenth it was confined to the area around Dublin known as the Pale. Outside of the Pale lived the 'mere Irish', who were Irish speakers. This is the history behind the term 'outside the Pale' used to denote someone who is out of favour. Even within the Pale bilingualism was common.

The turning point for Irish came in the sixteenth and seventeenth centuries when the native aristocracy was routed, killed or exiled. Subsequently, through the plantations of English and Scottish colonists as landowners in Irish-speaking districts, English became the language of law and commerce. While the majority of the population still spoke Irish as a native language, their numbers were halved by the middle of the nineteenth century through emigration and death as a result of the Famine. In the scramble for survival many now acquired English – from wherever possible and in whatever form that was available. This often resulted in mistakes that were left uncorrected and passed on. In Canon Peter O'Leary's recollections of his childhood in nineteenth century Ireland, he tells of a conversation he overheard between a serving boy and girl on his parent's farm:

> 'Con, she said in Gaelic … I have no speech now'. When the boy asked 'What else have you got' the girl said 'English'. When the boy asserted that surely English was speech she replied: 'If it was, surely people would understand it?'[1]

The girl further explains that she has 'Peter's English' and Seáinín-Philib's English only. In other words she has not learned English in a formal way, merely picking it up from neighbours. The English acquired under these circumstances was heavily marked by the Irish language. In the twentieth century James Joyce's Stephen Dedalus, the university-educated hero of *A Portrait of the Artist as a Young Man*, reflects on the differences between his speech and that of the English-born rector:

> His language, so familiar and so foreign, will always be for me an acquired speech. I have not made or accepted his words.[2]

The English that the Irish 'made' contained grammatical constructs, pronunciation, idioms and other language features that were carried over from Irish. These Irish English elements have been used by writers as markers of Irish nationality. They include:

- the use of the gerund plus 'after' to signify an action recently completed e.g. *I'm after finishing my dinner* for 'I have just finished my dinner'.
- the foregrounding of words for emphasis e.g. *Is it tired you are?*
- the use of 'and' recurrently for emphasis e.g. *They all arrived and I not expecting one of them.*

- excessive use of religious exclamations, benedictions and salutations e.g. *God between us and all harm.*
- the substitution of 'i' for 'e' and 'ay' for 'ea' e.g. *thin* for 'then' and *tay* for 'tea'.
- the rendering of words beginning with 's' as 'sh'.
- The use of Irish broad *f-* sound (a bilabial fricative) for the English *wh-* as in *phwat* for 'what'.
- calques or idioms directly translated from Irish e.g. 'the likes of'.
- Irish language words (usually anglicised in writing).

Whether the writer uses many or few of these Irish markers will depend to some extent on the education and class of the Irish character and the setting in which the dialogue occurs. The author who chooses to disclose a character's nationality through dialogue must be aware of the advantages and disadvantages of this strategy. The rendering of a character as comical may depend on the extent of the dialectal features used. However, care must be taken, in particular, in the portrayal of a major character, in case the character's role is devalued as a result of too great an emphasis on well known dialectal elements. Where comedy is intended, or where the role is a minor one, writers can freely choose to enhance the comic effect of an Irish character through the use of broken or mispronounced English, as well as a heavy dose of Irish English.

As language transfer was a lived experience for many nineteenth-century Irish in Australia we can expect that Australian literature will demonstrate this in the dialogue of Irish characters. We can also expect a reduction in Irish speech patterns towards a more standard English in twentieth-century literature, reflecting the end of bilingualism and an education system that ensures the successful acquisition of English and a move towards a more standard English. It would be unusual in Ireland today to encounter someone who speaks broken English or who makes major mistakes in English grammar or syntax.

In highlighting how the Irish speak English Australian authors follow a centuries-old tradition. It could be argued that in literature the Irish are defined by their way of speaking English to a greater extent than any other English-speaking race. This exclusive focus on the Irish voice is not confined to writing. In the eighteenth century, Jonathan Swift noted that the 'defects' in English and Scottish English did not affect the speaker's reputation:

> whereas, what we call the Irish Brogue is no sooner discovered, than it makes the deliverer, in the last degree, ridiculous and despised; and from such a mouth, an Englishman expects nothing but bulls, blunders and follies.[3]

The Irish language was the chief culprit in producing poor English expression in Ireland. Swift even warned landlords against learning Irish in order to become better landlords:

> It may possibly be so: But, I think, they should be such who never intend to visit England, upon pain of being ridiculous. For I do not remember to have heard of any man that spoke Irish, who have not the accent upon his tongue, easily discernible to an English ear.[4]

So it would appear that in the eighteenth century the Irish dialect of English was an object of ridicule, and the speaking of the Irish language was detrimental to English speakers with social aspirations. Of course these things would have mattered only when the Irish attempted to move in circles where standard English was expected. Swift was clearly sensitive to the fact that an Irish accent may adversely affect the social standing of the Anglo-Irish who, he claimed, had the 'misfortune of being born in Ireland' (although of English parents and with an education in England).[5] Swift used the term *brogue* to describe Irish English. The history of this word will demonstrate why it is such a useful word for a writer.

The word *brogue*, meaning a type of speech, is thought to have evolved as a result of the association of the speech of the Irish with the wearing of a particular type of shoe; the Irish for 'shoe' is *bróg*, anglicised as *brogue*. Consequently, a person who wears *brogues* might also speak with a *brogue*. Another possibility for the origin of *brogue* is the Irish word *barróg*, for which lexicographer Niall Ó Dónaill provides an initial meaning 'hug', but also a third meaning of: 'Brogue, impediment of speech.'[6] We can assume then that in the Irish language a person who has a speech impediment is said to speak with a *brogue*. Such a person would make many mistakes in early stage second language acquisition: the Irish person speaking English would speak with a *brogue*. If *barróg* rather than *bróg* is the origin of *brogue*, the disparagement in the term came from Irish speakers in the first place. This Irish language word that criticises attempts to acquire English, may have brought the term into the English language. From there the word may have developed to describe an Irish person speaking English, even if that speech was grammatically correct. The pejorative nature of the word remains in Ireland. Not surprisingly, it is a term rarely used by the Irish themselves, and the term *brogue* would not be used by an Irish writer except for satirical purposes.

It is the subtext of the word *brogue* that is important; however, this subtext originates from the word's etymology and its use over time. The term *brogue* has moved between being deprecatory and condescending, to mildly patronising. Whatever the author's intentions, the use of the term *brogue* sets an Irish character apart.

Irish names were carried throughout the country: the Shamrock Hotel in Gulgong, NSW.
HOLTERMANN COLLECTION, STATE LIBRARY OF NSW

The History of the Brogue

The *Oxford English Dictionary* provides a quotation from a Mrs Delaney in *Life & Correspondence in 1758* in which she describes a priest as being 'the quintessence of an Irish brogueneer'. There is a marked increase in entries for *brogue* in the *OED* from the nineteenth century, demonstrating both the popularity of the word and the increase of the Irish presence in England. While Famine emigrants and workers seeking seasonal employment made up the bulk of this presence in the mid nineteenth century, the Irish presence had already been noticed and noted in the highest circles. Following a number of insurrections in Ireland in the eighteenth century, England abolished the Irish Parliament and introduced the Act of Union in 1801 which brought political unification to the two countries. From then on Ireland was to be represented in the Parliament in London by twenty-eight Irish peers in the House of Lords and one hundred members of parliament in the House of Commons.[7] The Irish, however, had always set themselves apart from the English in terms of religion and language. Attempts at subjugation by the English had always been resisted. Political unification in the form of the Act of Union could only continue to point up the differences between the two peoples. Such was the impact of the arrival of the Irish into the hallowed halls of English administration that in 1878 the claim was that 'the very stones of Westminster Hall are saturated with Irish brogue'.[8] An Irish dialect of English was now operating at the highest levels of power.

According to historian Patrick O'Farrell, it was not until the 1830s that Irish immigrants moved to England in significant numbers. They were distinctive in their dress, clay pipes and odd hats and had 'a foreign-sounding English in the brogue'.[10] The social consequences of this immense and sudden presence of the Irish can be imagined. The strain on linguistic tolerance would also have increased substantially, English dialects being of concern to those who equated language with mindset.

In eighteenth-century England the prevailing theory was that the development of a national language would have a unifying effect on the country. The Scots language was condemned and warnings were given about the English spoken by the Irish, the Welsh, and the inhabitants of some districts in England who had words and phrases that those in authority did not understand. The answer was to have an official standard English. The Irish Parliamentarians of the time were mainly well-to-do, Protestant, and educated in England. We can presume that the English they spoke in Westminster was standard in syntax and grammar; nevertheless, they demonstrated in their speech that they were more Irish than English. The concern about brogue speech in high society may say more about Irish English politics than about the nature of speech; however, these are also linked.

We can see that the speech of the Irish in English society has been controversial on political, social and linguistic grounds. As many of Australia's nineteenth-century writers were English-born and raised, we can presume that they would have absorbed these views of the Irish and their language. Initially writing for an English readership, these authors would naturally draw upon accepted representation of the Irish character, but they could also draw from the rich source in Australia in the form of real life characters, both historical and living. The language of living Irish in Australia was the same language that had caused linguistic and social concerns in England. In the convict society in particular there would have been many rural Irish, who had probably never moved far from home before their transportation. Some of these convicts would have spoken Irish only, as that was the language of their community (as would have been the situation with later, free settlers). Those who spoke English may have used a heavy Irish English dialect or broken English.

The Irish/convict connection is characteristically Australian. The topic of language and Irish heritage takes on an extra edge in Australia, and likewise in Australian writing. The writer who comments on this provides an insight into the social concerns of the time. For example, in Mary Theresa Vidal's

Bengala or Some Time Ago (first published in 1860, but set in the 1840s) the character of an Australian nurse is represented by the use of religious oaths, the Irish exclamation *ochón* 'alas' (written as 'Och hon!') and the author's comment:

> and then followed a succession of Irish howls and exclamations in a hybrid tongue, made up between her Irish descent and the currency speech she had learnt in the colony. For 'nurse' was a currency woman, her parents being 'real' Irish emigrants, one of the first that ever came to Sydney.[10]

This passage indicates that Irish language words of emotion, such as ejaculations and exclamations, were passed down to second generation Australians. The passage also shows that English in Australia had deviated from standard English to the point of being criticised. In 1829 Edward Wakefield wrote from Sydney that the convicts ('our lowest class') had brought with them 'a peculiar language' and that this meant that 'pure English' was not 'the language of the colony'.[11] The social ramifications of a convict heritage, or in the case of the Irish, a suspected one, could be compounded by the use of recognisable Irishisms. This struggle for Irish respectability in Australia is the topic of Miles Franklin's novel *All That Swagger* (1943). The novel covers a hundred years in the lives of Irish-born Danny and Johanna Delacy and their Australian children. The family is faced with the language problem as the children grow up. Johanna decides against sending them to be educated at a convent school because 'the Roman Catholic creed and the brogue would be detrimental socially'.[12] She avoids being friendly with Mrs Wells, whose father had been a convict.[13] Johanna's own Irish background is a source of pride to her, but is also detrimental to her aspirations for her children. An example of this is when a powerful figure in the social circle that may hold Johanna's future daughter-in-law finds Johanna to be 'a kind little woman, but so *dreadfully* Irish'.[14] Johanna's husband, Danny, has found Johanna's own language prejudice amusing:

> You think yourself has less brogue than Hennessy, and I think I have less than you, but outsiders would lump us all together.[15]

These social and linguistic concerns would diminish for the Irish in Australia in succeeding generations. It is significant that it is only from the safe vantage point of Australian identity that those of Irish descent can view an Irish accent differently. Franklin, in using the theme of the Irish accent as a problematic social marker, is not typical of twentieth-century writers. Most twentieth-century Australian writers refer to the brogue in passing as an item of nostalgia. Some examples are Ruth Park's character Sister Theophilus in *The Harp in the South* (1948), who on meeting an old Irish woman is delighted to hear 'a real Irish voice' again, continuing, 'I haven't heard the real brogue since my father died'.[16] Later in the novel comes another memory of another dead father, 'God he had a tongue on him, sweet as honey with the brogue'.[17] In Lawson and Hickey's *Moira of Green Hills* (1950) the authors describe a character as having a 'deep brogue'. They depict this in the line 'But this is loike Oireland, this grane counthry'.[18] In this example the term *brogue* must be qualified by an example, because the comic aspect of the Irish accent is being emphasised. Not all twentieth-century Australian authors use the term *brogue* to describe an Irish character's speech pattern. Ruth Park describes a 'Grandad's purling Irish tones';[19] Criena Rohan comments on an Australian speech that has 'beauty, roughness, strange taciturn expressiveness' with 'overtones of Ireland',[20] and one of Thomas Keneally's characters has an 'Irish accent, uttered with the rich roll of the Milesian [native Irish] tongue'.[21] In the absence of the representative speech patterns, these references can still tap into the average reader's knowledge bank of the Irish sound. More importantly, when the author wishes to elevate an Irish character, an avoidance of direct representation of speech may be the best option.

Authorial devices for introducing Irish characters may also involve the use of a recognisably Irish first name such as Brigid or Paddy, or a common Irish surname such as Casey or Murphy, or a name beginning with O, such as O'Hara. This introduction is usually followed by a piece of dialogue that confirms the character's origins. The dialogue may involve a light or heavy use of Irish English dialectal elements. The choice often depends on whether the character is a major or minor one, the social class the character belongs to, his or her education, and the character's temperament. Authorial intervention is sometimes used to guide the reader in the interpretation of dialogue. For example, in chapter two of Joseph Furphy's *Such is Life* (1903), Tom Collins is joined by 'Dan O'Connell' from 'Armagh', who is a Catholic. An experienced reader will have deduced by these pointers of name, place of birth, and religion that this is an Irish character. Furphy further reinforces this, however, by rendering Dan's speech in heavy Irish English that carries a forewarning:

> While I complimented him on his erudition, he remarked, with amusing incompatibility of dialect and manner, 'Mebbe it's thrue fur ye, me father hed consitherable mains, so he hed; A har'ly ivver done a han's turn, furbye divarsion, to A come out here.[22]

The passage includes the Irish language idiom *is fíor duit* (it's true for you) in translation. Most of the vowel sounds are non-standard and have Scottish resonances in keeping with those influences on the Northern Ireland dialect of English. Furphy needs the reader to accept the major role that his character will play in the novel, and so intervenes to give the character stature. Of course, this device also gives the author stature in his reproduction of an authentic Armagh man in Australia.

In the 1956 novel *The Brown Land was Green*, the character Terence O'Callaghan is not introduced as Irish; however, his name and his opening lines are clear markers of his nationality:

> Sure and begorra it's green now, me girl … but this is August, the Colony's winter – almost spring – it'll be brown in a few months, and ye'll never believe it was ever green.[23]

Although the dialectal elements are light in this passage, the term 'sure and begorra' is another established national marker in writing of Irish nationality (although it is a term the Irish writer would avoid). A name and religious evocation at the beginning of *The Wild Colonial Girl* (1996) are also enough to introduce the reader to its Irish protagonist:

> Jaysus and Mary! Will you stop that cryin', Brigid? You'd think it was the end of the world.[24]

Even without the use of the traditionally Irish name *Brigid*, the Irishness of this passage is still present in the religious evocation 'Jaysus and Mary'. In the same way, and with no authorial comment or revealing name, the prostitute in the novel *The Fortunes of Richard Mahony* (1917), is clearly Irish:

> Even a weary old strumpet, propping herself against the doorway of the dancing-saloon, waved a tipsy hand and cried: 'Arrah, an' is it yerself, Purrdy, me bhoy! Shure an' it's bussin' ye I'd be afther – if me legs would carry me![25]

The Irish prostitute is not a stock character in Australian writing; however, Irish stock characters are often Catholic, unskilled, uneducated, or like the 'strumpet' in the previous piece, over-emotional. They occupy the lower ranks of Australian society and their role is to provide comic relief or local colour to the plot. In nineteenth-century Australia particularly, many Irish were in servile roles, owing to their poor immigrant background or their convict status. Language is often an indicator of class. Therefore writers will often use the language of real life to convey a character's background. The heavier the use of dialectal elements, the greater is the difficulty for the reader (or the hearer). It seems to be a basic human response to consider anyone who does not speak our language properly as defective in other areas such as hearing ability and intelligence.

Many nineteenth-century writers in Australia drew on the broad theme of the naïve English character arriving in the colony and undergoing character-forming adventures that involve meeting with a variety of Australian types. Readers at 'Home' would have found these adventures thrilling. The further away from ordinary life the characters were, the more exotic the adventure.

Not surprisingly, writers often dressed up their characters' dialogue accordingly. One example of this is the novel *Benbonuna, A Tale of the Fifties* (1860) which, by its title, is targeted at an Australian readership as well as the typical armchair English reader. In this novel Irish speech is represented by a heavy use of Irish English. For example:

> just put yez fut well in the shtirrup, shove your knee toight agin the flap, and kape yer toe out of his girths, an' then lift yerself clane into yes sate widout jerking an'whin yer feels all right I'll let go.[26]

In this passage the Irish stationhand, Mick, is helping a young Englishman to mount a horse. Irish English elements in Mick's speech include the substitution of 'i' for 'e' (*whin, agin*) 'ay' for *'ea'(clane, sate*) and the use of 'sh' when 's' is followed or preceded by a slender vowel in the word *shtirrup*. Irish language influence is also apparent in the absence of the voiceless *th* /θ/ in some words, as seen in this passage in the word widout. The Irish language does not have the /θ/ sound and consequently English words like *three* and *tree* are pronounced 'tree', even by many educated people and even today. The use of these dialectal elements in writing, in particular the vowel alterations, produces a comic effect when set against standard English. The more dialogue deviates from convention the funnier it becomes; as Maurice Charney explains:

> the speech of low characters tends to be unpredictable and outside the expectations of social decorum. It is vivid, colloquial, slangy, pungent, and wild. Talk is an expressive medium rather than one that communicates anything rational.[27]

Charney also claims that most comedy stems from 'low characters' who are classless but who are servants, 'misfits and outcasts' or 'exiles and escapees from the high and middle classes'. The character 'Mick' in the novel *Benbonuna* is a stationhand on a property in outback South Australia, and there are hints that he has a convict background. *Benbonuna* follows the fortunes of a young Englishman, Frank Heslop, who hopes to learn how to run a station of his own. Part of his learning is his exposure to the dangers of life in the bush and his interaction with a variety of characters from backgrounds that are vastly different to his. These are obstacles Frank needs to overcome in order to succeed in colonial Australia. His only weapon is his background, represented by his standard and educated English. As the novel progresses, Frank's ease with even the densest dialectal rendition is analogous with his ease in mastering other aspects of colonial Australia. For example, when the Aboriginal stockman 'Moses' asks him: 'Where you bin put 'em Peter? and where your "nantoo" thit down? You lose 'em?' He replies:

> 'No, they lost me, or, rather, Peter did, the infernal brute! He led me a nice dance, and I knocked up my own horse following him'.

Following this exchange the narrator of the novel points to Frank 'correctly guessing' that 'nantoo' was native for a horse'.[28] Of course Frank's superiority with language matches his social superiority. We do not laugh at Frank's language as we do at the language of Mick. Comedy also often points to those who do not know or practise social rules[29] and the lowly Mick instructing his social superior on how to mount a horse is amusing, more so when his dialect is so dense that the instructions would be difficult to follow.

Irish characters are often made comic because of their expressed emotionalism. An important social rule is that of maintaining control over one's emotions in public. Nineteenth-century critic Matthew Arnold compared the emotional temperament of the Celt with English steadiness, and while his views were debated at the time, his claim has some linguistic support when we consider the number of terms of abuse and endearment, oaths and ejaculations that were retained under the language shift (see Chapter Four).

Writers frequently choose language that emphasises excitability, grief or sentimentality to portray the Irish national type, usually for a comic effect. For example, on the Chinaman's Flat in the Victorian goldfields of the nineteenth century, Mary Fortune meets a number of Irish families who express themselves in a dense Irish English dialect when under stress. One such character is Mrs Denihy, who, distressed at being unable to find her child and husband, exclaims:

> Ow! ow! meilla murther! me babby's gone Paathrick! Paathrick! where are you at all at all ... Wirrastthrue! wirrasthrue! arrah dacent woman did you see e're a man and a babby rowlin' about anywheres. Arrah be all that's holy if that isn't himself coming home for all the world like a miller and a cradle on his back.[30]

The Irish language religious ejaculation *A Mhuire 's trua* 'oh Mary it is a pity' is anglicised here as *wirrasthrue*. The phrase *meilla murther* is an Irish English expression of intense emotion composed of the Irish word for 'a thousand', *míle*, and the English word *murder*. The ejaculation *arrah* is an anglicised form of *arú* 'alas'. The emotional state of this character is exaggerated through the use of repetition and exclamation marks as well as Irish and Irish English oaths. The comedy also lies in the unintelligibility of many of these Irish words to the average reader. Language is being used for its emotional effect and not to impart information. Nineteenth-century Irish characters in Australian literature use religious oaths in calling for help, in cursing someone or simply as an emotional response to a situation. For example, in the novel *Bengala*, the oaths 'by all the saints' and 'by my sowl and St Patrick'[31] are used as mild expletives. Twentieth-century Australian literature is less inclined to use a heavy Irish English dialect in the depiction of the Irish character, but the religious oath continues to be used as a defining characteristic of an Irish character. Examples include: 'By the Holy Passion of Christ',[32] 'Be the Holy Mother an' the Blessed Saints!', and 'Be Jases, Mary an' Joseph'.[33]

In general these Irish characters are minor characters whose absence would not greatly alter the plot. However, the Irish are characteristically known to be verbose and their experience with two languages has produced a vocabulary to match that verbosity, so writers looking to liven up their plot or dialogue can introduce a minor Irish character and be certain that this will reward. Writers who choose to develop Irish characters beyond the comic must employ different tactics to achieve this. The writer who wishes to elevate an Irish character may provide only a few, but yet significant, dialectal elements. Other forms of elevation include favourable authorial comment and references to, or the appearance of, the Irish language.

Notes

1 Peter Leary, *My Own Story*, Cork: The Mercier Press, 1970. 48.

2 James Joyce, *A Portrait of the Artist as a Young Man*, London: Granada Publishing, 1979. 172.

3 Jonathan Swift, 'On Barbarous Denominations in Ireland' in *A Proposal for Correcting the English Tongue Polite Conversation*, etc., Oxford: Basil Blackwell, 1964. 281.

4 ibid. 281.

5 'On Barbarous Denominations in Ireland'. 281.

6 Niall Ó Dónaill, *Foclóir Gaeilge-Béarla*, Baile Átha Cliath (Dublin): Oifig an tSoláthair, 1977.

7 Gearóid Ó Tuathaigh, *Ireland Before the Famine*, Gill and MacMillan, Dublin: 1972. 34.

8 *The Oxford English Dictionary:* Second Edition, J.A. Simpson and E.S.C. Weiner eds, Oxford: Clarendon Press, 1989. 573.

9 Patrick O'Farrell, *The Irish In Australia*, Sydney: University of New South Wales Press, 1987. 17.

10 Mary Theresa Vidal, *Bengala or Some Time Ago*, Sydney: New South Wales University Press, 1990. 242.

11 Sydney J Baker, *The Australian Language*, Melbourne: Sun Books, 1970. 3.

12 Miles Franklin, *All That Swagger*, London: Angus and Robertson, 1943. 70.

13 *All That Swagger*, 102.

14 ibid. 112.

15 ibid. 108.

16 Ruth Park, *The Harp in the South*, Sydney: Horwitz Publications, 1969. 132.

17 *The Harp in the South*. 195.

18 Will Lawson and Tom Hickey, *Moira of Green Hills*, Sydney: Australasian Publishing Company, 1950. 59.

19 Ruth Park, *Poor Man's Orange*, Sydney: Horwitz Publications, 1969. 113.

20 Criena Rohan, *Down by the Dockside*, London: Victor Gollancz Ltd, 1963. 174.

21 Thomas Keneally, *The Great Shame,* Sydney: Random House, 1998. 80.

22 Joseph Furphy, *Such is Life*, Sydney: Halstead Classics, 1999. 54.

23 Mavis Thorpe Clark, *This Brown Land Was Green,* London: William Heinemann Ltd, 1956. 8.

24 Ann Clancy, *The Wild Colonial Girl,* Sydney: Pan MacMillan, 1996. 3.

25 Henry Handel Richardson, *The Fortunes of Richard Mahony,* Sydney: The Discovery Press, 1968. 20.

26 Robert Bruce, *Benbonuna,* edition prepared by Rick Hosking, Adelaide: Flinders University of South Australia, 2002. 60.

27 Maurice Charney, *Comedy, High and Low,* London: Oxford University Press, 1987. 52–53.

28 *Benbonuna*. 27.

29 Arthur Asa Berger, *An Anatomy of Humor,* London: Transaction Publishers, 1998. 10.

30 Mary Fortune, *The Fortunes of Mary Fortune*, Melbourne: Penguin Books of Australia, 1989. 100.

31 *Bengala*. 190–191.

32 Leslie Haylen, *Big Red,* Sydney: Australasian Book Society, 1965. 19.

33 Frank Bruno, *Fury at Finnegan's Folly*, London: Robert Hale Limited, 1962. 35.

chapter four

Irish words in Australian writing

Érin go brách: Ireland forever

This chapter is a study of over 140 Irish words and nineteen phrases in use in Australian writing between 1829 and 2002. Not all words or phrases have been in use for the whole period, as the chronology of these Irish words shows both a standard vocabulary of Irish words and phrases used by Australian writers and a vocabulary limited to the nineteenth-century. The term 'standard' has been used to define words that have been used by more than one writer. When this use has spanned a significant period there is little doubt that a standard lexis exists.

The Glossary that is the outcome of this study of a range of Australian writing was prompted by a similar study that had Irish writing as its base and from which a Glossary was also developed.[1] As the studies are comparable, both glossaries provide useful insights into the similarities and differences in the occurrence of Irish language words in both Irish and Australian writing. The Glossary that resulted from the Irish study I will call the Irish Glossary to differentiate it from the Australian Glossary. The number of Australian writers in the twentieth and twenty-first centuries who have written on Irish themes or who use Irish characters is small. This could change in the twenty-first century and, in theory, a number of writers could emerge who choose different Irish words. For the purpose of this study, however, I have noted those words which appear to indicate a move from isolated borrowing to standard. The following table lists all words used by two or more writers in order of frequency of occurrence. The word is presented as it is written in Irish. Some entries include the form or forms the word usually takes in English. Not all forms have been included, but all are included in the Glossary. In addition, for the purpose of brevity the translations of the words do not always match

A St Patrick's Day march in Bega. At the top of the banner with the Celtic cross is the slogan 'Erin go bragh'

BICENTENNIAL COPYING PROJECT, STATE LIBRARY OF NSW

those provided in the Glossary. For example, the word *seonín* is translated as 'a flunkey'. The Glossary provides the historical meaning of the word as coming from the term John Bull.

Standard Australian lexis

Word	Meaning	Occurrences	Time span
ara as arrah, yerra,erra, etc.	'alas'	26	1840–2001
Muire as musha, wisha,wirrah,etc	'Mary', 'alas'	21	1829–1999
spraoi as spree	'a prolonged drinking bout'	21	1853–1997
spailpín as spalpeen, etc.	'a migratory labourer', 'a lout'	18	1840–1998
garsún as gossoon	'a boy'	17	1845–1948
bean sí as banshee	'a fairy woman'	16	1874–2001

cailín as colleen	'a girl'	14	1829–1988
caoineadh as keening	'lamentation'	12	1865–2001
poitín as poteen	'illicit whiskey'	11	1900–2002
mo mhuirnín as mavourneen	'my darling'	11	1867–1995
sail éille as shillelagh	'a cudgel'	10	1806–1949
a leanbh as alannah	'oh child/darling'	10	1845–1963
a chuisle as acushla etc.	'oh pulse'	9	1845–1963
amadán as omadhaun etc.	'a fool'	9	1867–1950
síbín as shebeen etc.	'an unlicensed premises selling alcohol	8	1908–2001
mo chroí as machree etc.	'my heart'	8	1857–1945
straoil as streel	'a slovenly woman', 'wandering aimlessly'	7	1921–1946
bóithrín as boreen	'a small road'	7	1855–1999
ochón as ochone, etc.	'alas'	7	1840–1962
a stór as asthore etc.	'oh treasure'	6	1882–1943
bróg as brogue	'a shoe'	6	1840–1986
dúidín as dudeen etc.	'a short smoking pipe'	6	1845–1998
Éire go brách as Erin go bragh etc.	'Ireland forever'	6	1926–1999
uisce beatha	'whiskey'	4	1978–2002
a ghrá as agrah	'oh love'	4	1840–1999
a mhic as avic	'oh son'	4	1867–1928
call	'right, claim'	4	1889–1949
cipín as kip	'a short stick'	4	1928–1965
clábar	'mud'	4	1859–1945
diabhal	'devil'	4	1849–2002
buachaill	'a boy'	3	1867–1998
fág an bealach as faugh a ballagh	'clear the way'	3	1854–1998
fáilte	'welcome'	3	1845–1998
gob	'mouth'	3	1928–1948
paltóg as polthogue	'a blow, a thump'	3	1840–1867
sagart as soggarth	'a priest'	3	1919–1998

scailp as scalpeen	'a fissure in a rock', a rude cabin'	3	1998–1999
seamróg as shamrock	'a three leafed small plant'	3	1921–1999
tráithnín as traneen	'a piece of straw'	3	1845-1919
aisling	'a vision poem'	2	1943, 1999
bastún as bostoon	'a lout'	2	1906, 1908
mo bhrón as mavrone	'alas'	2	1945, 1999
cáibín as caubeen	'an old hat'	2	1859, 1926
cál ceannan as colcannon	mashed potatoes/leeks etc	2	1916, 1999
céilí	'a dance'	2	1967, 1998
Dia	'God'	2	1961, 1998
feis	'a festival'	2	1943, 1998
gaimbín as gombeen	'a usurer'	2	1859, 1991
laí as loy	'a spade'	2	1945, 1998
leipreachán as leprechaun	'a little fairy man'	2	1919, 1965
púca as pooka	'a ghost'	2	1945, 2001
rapaire as rapparee	'a highway man'	2	1900, 1908
Sasanach	'Englishman'	2	1919, 1998
seoinín as shoneen	'a flunkey'	2	1921, 1998
spleodar as splother etc.	'cheerfulness'	2	1921, 1928
taoiseach	'Irish prime minister'	2	1991, 1998

These Irish words occurring in Australian writing may be divided into the categories of interjections, and terms of abuse and endearment, because these words of emotion, above all, are chosen by writers as representative of Irish expression. The speed with which the Irish transferred from speaking Irish to English is astounding when viewed from today's vantage point. This speed may have influenced the retention of Irish words of emotion. It takes some time to master the subtleties inherent in exclamatory words: consider the difference between 'ah no!' and 'oh no!'. It has also been suggested that the Irish retained their emotive words because they had a greater need of them. James Clark noted this in his comparison of language transfer in Ireland and Scotland:

> In Ireland alone were terms of endearment, ejaculations of lament, etc. retained ... it is due to the more demonstrative and passionate temperament of the Irish, as opposed to the more reticent nature of the Shetlanders.[2]

The suggestion that Irish words of an emotional nature were retained in the English of Ireland because of the emotional nature of the Irish is plausible. Some of the Irish who came to Australia apparently exhibited emotion to a greater extent than other migrant or transported groups. For example in 1822 it was noted that the Irish transportees had a greater emotional response to 'the separation from their native country' than others.[3] Patrick O'Farrell comments on the 'shrieks, prayers, blessings and lamentations' from Irish families on Cork wharf in 1840 as a group of emigrants was leaving for Australia.[4] What is certain is that Irish words of emotion have formed the standard vocabulary of Anglo-Irish writing spanning two centuries. These words of abuse, interjection and endearment are also standard in Australian writing of the same period. The Glossary of the Australian study shows that almost one-third of the words in use are words of an emotional nature.

The following words found in Australian writing also occur in Irish writing and so offer the opportunity for comparison. The tables below demonstrate the frequency of occurrence of Irish interjections in Australian writing and the time span in which they occur.

Interjections

Word	Meaning	Occurrences	Time Span
ara as arrah, yerra, erra, etc.	'alas'	26	1840–2001
Muire as musha, wisha,wirrah,etc.	'Mary', 'alas'	21	1829–1999
ochón as ochone, etc.	'alas'	7	1840–1962
diabhal	'devil'	4	1849–2002
mo bhrón as mavrone	'alas'	2	1945, 1999

The word *ara* is the most frequently used Irish word in Australian writing. Diarmaid Ó Muirithe translates it as 'Ah! Indeed!' He finds it in the forms 'aru', 'airiú', 'arrah', 'arra', 'arah', 'eroo', 'rhoo', 'yerra' and 'yerrou'. The Australian study finds similar forms but with the addition of 'gerrah' from 1840. However no 'oo' variants were found in the Australian study.

In the Australian Glossary the words *ara* and *Muire* are popular Irish interjections in use in Australian writing. These words are equally as popular with Irish writers, except that the word *Muire* has a greater frequency of occurrence over *ara*. The word *Muire* is 'Mary' the name of the Blessed Virgin. The English spelling of the word includes forms such as 'musha', 'wisha' and 'wirreh'. The first two examples are possibly evidence of the development of the word over time where the middle 'r' sound was replaced by an 'sh' sound. The forms beginning with 'w' are evidence of the pronunciation of the word under the rules of lenition. For example *Muire* is pronounced roughly 'mwirreh' but the term *a Mhuire* 'oh Mary' is pronounced 'ah wirreh'. Four forms of the term *Muire* were found in the Australian study that were not found in the Irish studies: 'murra', 'wisher', 'ouisha' and 'isha'. The writers do not appear to have been influenced by the conventional spelling of these words. As such, they may represent the sounds heard in Australia. The form 'wisher' has an intrusive 'r' that may have been influenced by Australian English. Another variation in the Australian collection of the word *Muire* is that the forms 'wirra', 'wirrah', 'whirra' are found through both centuries, whereas the central 'r' form had only one occurrence in the twentieth century in the Irish study. In Anglo-Irish writing the spelling 'wisha' became standard from the second half of the twentieth century, but there is no such standardisation in Australian spelling.

Australian writers use these terms more often than Irish writers, e.g. twenty-six uses of *ara* to fourteen in the Irish study and twenty-one uses of *Muire* and seventeen in the Irish study. As Irish characters in Australian writing are often minor players, the Australian writer has, perhaps, a greater imperative to be efficient in the use of terminology to mark that character's nationality; as long established national markers, the words *ara* and *musha* or *wisha* serve that purpose well. The Irish writer too uses the terms as markers, but more as signs of a character's rural origins; the remote and rural parts of Ireland being the repositories of the Irish language and so more likely to retain Irish language expression in English speech.

The Irish writer chooses Irish language terms of abuse above terms of endearment. Terms of abuse are equally popular in Australian writing, as the following table demonstrates.

Terms of Abuse

Word	Meaning	Occurrences	Time span
spailpín as spalpeen etc.	'a migratory labourer', 'a lout'	18	1840–1998
amadán as omadhaun etc.	'a fool'	9	1867–1950
straoil as streel	'a slovenly woman', 'wandering aimlessly'	7	1921–1946
bastún as bostoon	'a lout'	2	1906, 1908
gaimbín as gombeen	'a usurer'	2	1859, 1991
rapaire as rapparee	'a highway man'	2	1900, 1908
Sasanach	' Englishman'	2	1919, 1998
seoinín as shoneen	'a flunkey'	2	1921, 1998

The most frequently used term of abuse in the Irish study was the word *gaimbín;* however, it comes low in the Australian table. The social conditions of Ireland produced the term. The 'gombeen men' were village usurers charging sometimes in excess of 40 per cent interest in areas that had no shops or bank. The word in modern Irish writing has moved beyond that of 'usurer', and can stand for someone who is dull or unsophisticated, that is, from a rural rather than an urban background. Significantly the Australian uses of *gaimbín* are those of an Irish rather than an Australian setting. Irish-born William Kelly uses the term in 1859 in his *Life in Victoria* as a description of a usurer in Australia. He glosses the term as: 'Gombeen man is an Irish character – a village usurer'. Kelly is using the term in its original sense, whereas in Ireland it has developed into a general term of contempt. Australian poet Vincent Buckley uses the term in a Dublin poem written while he was living there. This avoidance by the Australian writer of what is the most popular Irish term of abuse in Irish writing may be due to an awareness that the abusive nature is specific to Irish conditions and so cannot be transported.

By contrast, the Irish writer ceased to use the term *spailpín* as a word of abuse in the twentieth century (there were only five occurrences in the Irish study), while it occurs seventeen times in the Australian study. As a term of abuse, however, the last usage by an Australian author in this study was 1962. In Ireland, the abuse associated with the word *spailpín* originated when landless men were forced to travel for work outside of their own communities. These migratory workers would naturally attract suspicion in closed and settled communities. The fact that the term is used three times as much in Australian writing may reflect a fear among unskilled Irish people in Australia of a return to poverty. Most of the Australian entries for *spalpeen* show the word as meaning a despicable person. The 1865 entry from Ellen Davitt's *Force and Fraud* includes the gloss 'a low or mean fellow'. The 1960 entry from Elizabeth O'Connor's *The Irishman* refers to an old Irish woman in Australia who shouts abuse at the passing schoolchildren. Two entries use the term in its traditional sense of a migratory labourer. William Kelly, in *Life in Victoria,* uses the word *spalpeen* when comparing how passengers between Melbourne and the Bendigo goldfields were often obliged to walk because of the condition of the roads with how Irishmen worked their passage to Dublin by driving the horses for the canal barges along the banks. In effect they would have been as well off if they had simply walked the whole way. Thomas Keneally also uses the term in its original sense in 1998 in *The Great Shame.* This frequency of use in Australian writing may then mirror the frequency in which the word *spalpeen* was used in the Irish Australian speech community.

The use of the word *ropaire*, anglicised as *rapparee* in two Australian novels contrasts significantly with the Irish occurrences. The Irish study found the word *rapparee* in 1842 and in Joyce's *Ulysses*, and in both cases the abusive nature was mild. The Australian entries have a stronger connotation. This is, perhaps, because the banditry and thievery associated with the term *rapparee* was stronger in the folk memory of Australia because of the bushrangers in the last half of the nineteenth century. Of course, Australian writers may have preferred this Irish term of abuse because of the way it sounds or the way it looks.

Finally, the Australian uses of the term *straoil*, anglicised as *streel*, are worth commenting on because of a divergence from the standard use of the term in Irish writing. The Irish study showed five uses of the term meaning 'a ragged person' and four uses of the term as a verb meaning 'to straggle'. The Australian study has four uses of the term where it refers to a person in the same sense as the Irish use. The entries for the word as a verb differ slightly in Australian writing. The 1845 entry's context is a dispute over low wages and a threat to go away and compare wages on other properties. The response is 'If you go sthreeling about looking for more wages ...', where the word implies more a sense of causing trouble than of aimlessly wandering or straggling. The Irish study found no use of *straoil* other than as a term of abuse for a female and as a verb meaning 'to straggle'. The 1946 Australian entry, however, refers to 'a streel of clouds' and this more poetic use fits Ó Muirithe's 'A string of (beads, etc.)'. Katherine Prichard's 'a streel of clouds', however, occurs in a general and non-Irish setting. These Irish terms of abuse, in the main, however, operate as words in an Irish Australian setting and so reflect this new social setting.

Terms of endearment

Word	Meaning	Occurrences	Time span
garsún as gossoon	'a boy'	17	1845–1948
cailín as colleen	'a girl'	14	1829–1988
mo mhuirnín as mavourneen	'my darling'	11	1867–1995
a leanbh as alannah	'oh child/darling'	10	1845–1963
a chuisle as acushla etc.	'oh pulse'	9	1845–1963
mo chroí as machree etc.	'my heart'	8	1857–1945
a stór as asthore etc.	'oh treasure'	6	1882–1943
a ghrá as agrah	'oh love'	4	1840–1999
a mhic as avic	'oh son'	4	1867–1928
buachaill	'a boy'	3	1867–1998
sagart as soggarth	'a priest'	3	1919–1998

The terms *cailín*, 'a girl' and *garsún*, 'a boy' have been included in this list as terms of endearment because they are generally used in this sense in both Australian and Irish writing. These terms have a greater number of occurrences in Australian writing than in Irish writing, with Australian uses of *cailín* doubling the number of those found in the Irish study. In addition, *garsún* appears in the Australian study six times more than in the Irish study.

In Irish writing the term *cailín*, usually anglicised as *colleen*, may be used to convey a kind of innocence or artlessness; it is also mildly patronising or mocking. This, of course, is an extension of the word's meaning in an English setting, as in Irish it is simply the word for 'a girl'. In an English language setting the anglicised *colleen* evokes a rustic image of an Irish peasant girl. In twentieth-century Irish writing the use of the word *colleen* often points more to a lack of sophistication in the user of the word than the girl in question. In Australian writing the word *colleen* functions as a straightforward mark of nationality and as an endearment. It is not used in a satirical sense. For example the 1961 entry in the Australian Glossary for *cailín* reads: 'Steele Rudd's mother was Mary Green, a colleen from Roscommon'. The term is used here to mark the difference between Steele Rudd, the quintessential Australian novelist, author of the 'classic' *Dad and Dave* stories, and his marked Irish background, Roscommon being a county in the west of Ireland and therefore closer to traditional Irish culture than counties on the eastern side of the country.

In the novel *Pierce O'Grady's Daughter* the endearment *colleen* operates as such, but is also used as a code word. It adds to the dramatic plot in the novel when as a code word it is misinterpreted, and so sets off a misunderstanding between the central lovers of the novel.[5] The 1988 entry is from Eric Willmot's *Pemulwuy The Rainbow Warrior*, a story of the effects of the establishment of a penal colony in Australia from the indigenous population's point of view. An Irish convict character uses the Irish endearment to his Aboriginal lover: 'Listen my colleen, there is hope'. The use of this most intimate Irish word in an Australian setting not only confirms the Irishman's emotional commitment to this woman but is a reminder that they both share the experience of language loss at the hands of the British.

The word *garsún* (anglicised as *gossoon*) is a word used to describe a young boy and sometimes a boy who is a helper or servant. It comes from the French word *garçon*. As the term usually describes a young boy, it is used in the sense of an endearment and does not carry other connotations in Ireland. The greater use of the term in Australian writing comes from its extra value as a mark of nationality, usually of the speaker. For example the first entry in the Australian glossary sees the term operating alongside other cultural markers: 'And oughtn't I to know him whin we used to be gossoons together playing at hurley in ould Ireland'. The term *gossoon* is confirmation of how long the speaker has known the 'him' involved and how they share the same cultural background. This kind of intimate knowledge can be used as a weapon, as in the 1865 entry where the term *gossoon* is used to bring an Irish magistrate down to size in an Australian court: 'I've known ye since ye were a bit of a ragged gossoon'. In this case the magistrate's social standing is threatened by the knowledge that his background is one of uneducated Irish peasantry. The popularity of the terms *cailín* and *garsún* in Australian writing (in their anglicised forms) may be due to the sound of the words and the fact that they are terms that have operated in the English language for a long time; the Australian 1829 entry for *colleen* is only one year later than the first entry of the word in the *OED*.

The next endearment of significance in the Australian study is *a/mo mhuirnín* 'oh/my darling', anglicised as *avourneen* or *mavourneen*. The use of Irish terms of endearment in Irish and Australian writing differs significantly with the term *mavourneen*; the Australian usage is almost double the Irish usage. The reason for this is a change in circumstances in Ireland that made the word unpopular for Irish writers. In Ireland the word became popular in English in the context of a song, 'Kathleen Mavourneen', a nineteenth-century song recorded by the famous Irish tenor Count John McCormick at the turn of the twentieth century. Before that, however, it had strong associations with the American Civil War. The first verse of the song 'Kathleen Mavourneen' is:

> Kathleen, Mavourneen, the grey dawn is breaking,
> The horn of the hunter is heard on the hill;
> The lark from her light wing the bright dew is shaking;
> Kathleen, Mavourneen, What! slumbering still?
> Oh! hast thou forgotten how soon we must sever?
> Oh! hast thou forgotten, this day we must part;
> It may be for years, and it may be forever?
> Oh! why art thou silent, thou voice of my heart?
> It may be for years, and it may be forever?
> Oh! why art thou silent, Kathleen, Mavourneen?

The Irish study shows only one use in the twentieth century, in James Joyce's *Ulysses*. Joyce used Irish words for specific effects. His use of the term *mavourneen* is to satirise the stultifying provincialism of aspects of traditional Irish culture.[6]

The term *mavourneen* is avoided by the Irish writer because of its overuse and its mainly nineteenth-century sentimental links. The overuse of Irish words of endearment in nineteenth-century texts encouraged their use in comic situations, with the result that, for the Irish, they became associated with stage Irishry. Irish writers in the twentieth century have avoided using the term *a/mo mhuirnín* for the reason outlined by G.L. Brook:

> When variety artists want to make fun of the speech of any group of people, they choose a few easily recognisable characteristics, which have become traditional. Members of these groups try to avoid the features which are frequently satirised.[7]

The Australian writer has no such restrictions in the use of the term. As a result the endearment *mo mhuirnín* 'my darling' as *mavourneen* could conceivably be used by Australian writers today.

Religion and Superstition

Word	Meaning	Occurrences	Time span
caoineadh as 'keen', 'keening'	lamentation (for the dead)	12	1865–2001
bean sí as banshee	'a fairy woman'	12	1874–2001
diabhal	'devil'	4	1849–2002
Dia	'God'	2	1961, 1998
leipreachán as leprechaun	'a little fairy man'	2	1919, 1965
púca	'a ghost'	2	1945, 2001

The anglicised words *banshee*, *keen* and *leprechaun* are Irish words that are well established in English, which accounts for their popularity as markers of Irish nationality in Australian writing. We could expect these words to be avoided by modern Irish writers, as some endearments and terms of abuse have been. While the word *leprechaun* was not covered in the Irish study, the words *banshee* and *keen* were. The Irish usage of *banshee* equals the Australian usage, and there are two more uses of the word *keen/keening* in the Irish study. Irish writers have not avoided these words, but rather have extended their possibilities. For example, Christy Brown uses the term *banshee* as an adjective in the 1970 novel *Down All the Days*: 'the ice-cream man rumbled down the street blowing his banshee horn'.[8] The word *keen* is no longer Irish or Ireland-specific and has developed from a term for a form of lamentation over the dead to a general term for heavy or prolonged crying. Of course in Irish mythology the *banshee's* crying outside a window heralded the death of someone inside, and so both words feed on each other as sources of horror and fear. The Irish study showed the use of *keen* both in its universal sense of crying and also in its specific Irish sense of a lamentation over the dead. The Australian uses include two where the word operates outside of its traditional locale: 'keening casuarinas' in Miles Franklin's *All That Swagger*, and 'the keening of insects' in Michael Meehan's *The Salt of Broken Tears*. Perhaps because Australian writers have not lived in the environment where the word's superstitious connotations were established they have been free to develop its poetic possibilities. In this case, the word as sound can prevail over the word as meaning.

In Jill Blee's novel *The Liberator's Birthday*, Irish language words and phrases are a reminder that this Irish community in Ballarat maintains a world view that was formed in Ireland. This includes an emotional response to the supernatural and the power of religion in the guise of the local priest. His curse *chun an diabhal leat* – 'to the devil with you' – is taken very seriously in the dangerous world of the Ballarat mines in the nineteenth century. Another example of the connection between the Irish language and the supernatural is in the novel *The Emerald Whaler*, the story of the rescue of the Fenian prisoners off the coast of Western Australia by an American ship. The Fenian John Boyle O'Reilly has escaped to America previously and is helping to organise to rescue his remaining comrades. He decides not to go to the wharf to see the rescue ship the *Catalpa* on its way in case he is seen by informers who would then give the plot away. He sends instead a religious blessing for a safe voyage:

> He had entrusted the farewell message to Devoy – a slip of paper with the words: 'Go gcuiridh Dia an t-a'dh ort, Captain Anthony. Go soirbhi Dia dhuit.' And the bold signature: John Boyle O'Reilly.'

Devoy is obliged to translate the message for the ship's captain. The expectation is that these Irish language blessings will be the tie that binds the Fenians in America with those in Australia until they are physically reunited through the efforts of the ship's captain. As the captain is the only one on board to know the real intention of the voyage (to outward appearances the ship is a whaler) the Irish language blessings on this piece of paper in his pocket would maintain his sense of purpose. These Irish language words associated with religion and superstition are part of the standard lexis of the Irish and the Australian writer because they represent the mindset of the Irish. Other Irish language words in writing represent the image of the Irish as demonstrated in the table below.

Clothing and Accessories

Word	Meaning	Occurrence	Time span
sail éille as shillelagh	'a cudgel'	10	1840–1949
bróg as brogue	'shoe'	6	1840–1986

dúidín as doodeen etc.	'a short pipe'	6	1845–1998
cáibín as caubeen	'an old hat'	2	1859, 1926
laí as loy	'a spade'	2	1945, 1998

Patrick O'Farrell claims that the nineteenth-century Irish dressed distinctively: 'clay pipes, odd hats'.[9] The 1847 entry in the Glossary for the word *dúidín* is Alexander Harris's description of the motley dress of 'the very lowest class' in New South Wales, where 'the *dudeen* (a pipe with the stem reduced to three, two, one or half an inch) was in everybody's mouth' (see illustration on page 28). The group in question was a mixture of English, Irish, Scots and 'several foreigners'. This indicates that the distinctive Irish smoking pipe (and its name) was a general feature of the colony, and not confined to the Irish community. The word *dúidín* has two more occurrences in the Australian study than in the Irish study.

The anglicised word *shillelagh* did not feature in the Irish study, but has a high frequency rate in the Australian study. Ó Muirithe explains that it was a cudgel used in faction fighting in eighteenth- and nineteenth-century Ireland. It derives from the word *sail* 'a cudgel' and the genitive of the word for 'a thong' by which the cudgel was tied to the wrist. The 1859 entry in the Glossary has a background of the use of the *shillelagh* in the scramble for the unwanted possessions of newly arrived migrants. The 1949 entry from Ruth Park's *Poor Man's Orange*, 'you would have thought they had parked their shillelaghs in the porch', sees the word operating in an iconic sense. The 'they' are the congregation at Mass singing the hymn 'Faith of Our Fathers' with great emotion. The word *shillelagh* identifies this group as being Irish.

Another word associated with rural Ireland is *bróg*, 'a shoe'. The Irish study found a development in meaning for this word from that of inferior peasant footwear to the respected and sturdy footwear of the middle class hill climber. The Australian entries are notable for the forms *brogueens* and *brogans*. These are forms not found in the Irish study. Ó Muirithe, however, provides *brogueen* but not *brogan*. The Irish diminutive *án* is evident in the spelling *brogan* and this form of the diminutive of *bróg* may be a dialect word captured from Irish English speech in Australia or, as the entry for *brogans* is a twentieth-century entry, a change in the pronunciation of the suffix of *bróigín* over time.

Food and Drink

Word	Meaning	Occurrences	Time span
poitín	'illicit whiskey'	11	1900–2002

Poitín, illicit whiskey, being made in Connemara, Ireland.
WELCH COLLECTION, ULSTER MUSEUM, BELFAST

síbín as shebeen	'a place where drink is sold without a licence'	8	1908–2001
uisce beatha	'whiskey'	4	1978–2002
cál ceannan as colcannon	mashed potato, kale and leek	2	1916, 1999

Migrants to a new country bring a number of additions to the existing culture, including their own preferences in food and drink. The Irish brought the method and skill of making illicit whiskey to Australia. The traditional Irish method of whiskey making leaves out the distillation process, and the resultant *poitín* is very powerful and dangerous. This word has as its root *poit* 'a pot';

means 'little pot', the vessel that holds the product. The illicit nature of the production, and the potency of the whiskey and its effects, make this a useful word for both the Irish and Australian writer. Complementary to the word *poitín* is the *síbín*. Again, the illicit nature of the *shebeen*, operating outside of regulations, has literary potential, and both Irish and Australian writers exploit this potential. In Australia, as in Ireland, the keeping of a *shebeen* was often the only source of income for widows.[10] The 2000 entry in the Australian glossary for *síbín* has Ned Kelly's widowed mother buying a piece of land because it is near a road, offering commercial potential for her *shebeen*. The social conditions for some Irish in Australia in the nineteenth century were similar to those of the west of Ireland where isolation, poverty and a disdain for a 'foreign' law provided reason enough for acting illegally.

The four uses of the spelling *uisce beatha* for 'whiskey' in the Australian

Melbourne's Archbishop Daniel Mannix at the opening of a parish hall in Oakleigh, Victoria, in 1918, beneath the slogan 'Ireland Forever'.
MELBOURNE DIOCESAN HISTORICAL COMMISSION

study are another example of the Australian writer being unaware of a change in usage of an Irish word. The Irish study showed the term occurring in the twentieth century only in *Ulysses*. All but one of the Australian entries show the word elevated in its italicisation as well as in the use of Irish orthography. The exception is from Irish-born Joe O'Sullivan who uses the older spelling of *uisge*. It could be argued that O'Sullivan already elevates the word in this didactic piece. The Australian uses are also didactic in asserting the Irish origins of the word *whiskey*. Most Irish readers would know that the word *whiskey* is the Irish word *uisce*. Irish writers also avoid using the Irish word because of its use in nineteenth-century writing and because, with the commercialisation that has established the word *whiskey*, the use of the term *uisce beatha* would be counterproductive. The Australian entries begin in 1978, and so the Australian use of the word may signify an increase in interest in Irish matters as a result of the 'Troubles' and a wish to promote to Australian readers the Irish language and its contribution to English.

These Irish words of emotion, superstition, and food and drink form a standard vocabulary for the Australian writer as they do for the Irish writer. There are some differences, as has been seen, in the frequency of occurrence or slight changes of meaning. The greatest difference in the occurrence of Irish words in Australian writing is in the extended use of an Irish word in the Australian environment or Irish words that have altered over time, and which operate as slang words. Some of these will be discussed in the Glossary, which follows this chapter.

The Sydney department store Mark Foy's used the slogan 'faugh a ballagh' (fág an bealach) meaning 'clear the way' to advertise its 1902 St Patrick's Day holiday.

Slogans

Word	Meaning	Occurrence	Time span
fág an bealach as faugh-a-ballagh	'clear the way'	3	1854–1998
Éire go brách as Erin go bragh, Erin go brách	'Ireland forever'	6	1926–1999

Irish political slogans have also found greater currency in Australian writing than in Irish writing. For example the slogan *fág an bealach,* 'clear the way', is found mainly in nineteenth-century Australian writing, but Thomas Keneally uses it in 1998 in *The Great Shame*. Keneally's reference is to a nineteenth century poem with the title 'Faugh-a-Ballagh'. The term in this anglicised form apparently spread from its use in eighteenth-century faction fighting in Ireland to its use by the Royal Irish Fusiliers regiment in the British army during the Peninsular War and the Irish Brigade in the American Civil War. The Australian entries for this term, however, show it in use outside of both the faction fighting and military settings. Specifically, the Glossary entry for 1854 shows it being used as an adjective: 'poor Faugh-a-ballagh savage!' The 1859 entry is of author William Kelly's use of the term (without any explanation) as a retort, meaning 'say no more': 'faugh-a-ballagh was the shout of the Double-rose Cork manufacturer'. The historical work *Two Years in Australia* talks about the 'Bendigo Faugh a Ballachs' as a term given to 'thieves'.[11] These Australian entries point to a more general use of the term *fág a bealach* than that of faction fighting or as a military term. In 1902 the term *Faugh a Ballagh* written above a racing car was used in a St Patrick's day advertisement for the Sydney retailer Mark Foy's.[12] As there is no translation provided, we must conclude that the phrase was in general currency in Irish Australian circles at that time.

The other slogan is *Éire go brách* – 'Ireland forever' – which has six occurrences in the Australian study, but none in the Irish study. The term is anglicised often as *Erin go bragh*. The earliest recorded use of the term in Ireland appears to be as a song of exile in the 1795 'The Exiled Irishman's Lamentation', an anthology of songs promoting the Belfast-based political group the United Irishmen. It became the slogan of this group, and their 1798 rebellion against British rule in Ireland resulted in hundreds of prisoners being transported to Australia. *Erin go Bragh* was the name of a nineteenth century passenger ship travelling between Liverpool and America. It was also the name of a badly run ship that carried Irish emigrants to Queensland under the assisted passage scheme of the Queensland Immigration Society in the 1860s, resulting in the loss of 51 lives.[13] In July 1918 it was the slogan for a banner at the opening of a parish hall in Oakleigh, Victoria by Archbishop Daniel Mannix (see page 61).[14]

The slogans *fág a bealach* and *Éire go brách* are words of emotion in the same way as interjections, terms of abuse and terms of endearment, but they also served to bolster the political aspirations of Irish exiles in America and Australia. They are unlikely to occur in modern Irish or Australian writing except in historical works (and these are more likely to be Australian because Australians are more interested in Irish history than Irish writers are in Irish Australian or Irish American history).

Nineteenth-century Words

Word	Meaning	Occurrences	Time span
an ea? as inyagh	'is it?'	1	1882
bó as vo	'alas'	1	1882
breacast as breqquest	'breakfast'	1	1845
cóisir as coshering/cothering	'gossiping'	1	1867
b'fhéidir sin as bothershion	'perhaps so'	1	1867
hububú as hubabuboo	'wailing'	1	1829
míle murder as meila murther	'thousand murders'	1	1882
paltóg as polthogue	'a blow, thump'	3	1840–1867

The Irish study found a range of words confined to nineteenth-century writing that, perhaps, represent a stage of bilingualism in the country. The Australian study has found a smaller number of these nineteenth-century words. Of the words in this list only *bó* as 'vo' was found in the Irish study. All of these words, however, are in Ó Muirithe's collection of Irish words in use in Irish English, so they may represent Irish English as spoken in nineteenth-century Australia. These words are mainly from works supposedly based on true experiences, such as the journals kept by Mary Fortune of her visits to the Victorian goldfields and the account of the adventures of the convict Ralph Rashleigh. Presumably the words these writers chose were heard in the Australian Irish speech community of the time, and so the study of them is of linguistic and socio-historical value. For example, in the novel *Fifty Years Ago,* the Irish word *breacast* as 'breqquest' is used instead of English *breakfast*. Today the standard Irish word for 'breakfast' is *bricfeasta*. The form *breacast* may be an older form of the word or from a particular dialect. Its capture in Australian print is significant.

The word *paltóg* has three occurrences in the Australian Glossary, but none in the Irish Glossary. Ó Muirithe provides many examples, so it is clearly a popular word in Irish English speech. His literary examples are of the word being used in the sense of 'a heavy shower or rain'. Ó Muirithe also points to a similar English dialect word *polt*, *pelt*, meaning 'strike'. The Australian use of the Irish word may have been reinforced by the presence of the English dialect word. Another word that may have been influenced by an English word is *cóisir*. The entries in the Australian Glossary are from Charles De Boos' *Fifty Years Ago* and the words *cothering* and *coshering* are used alongside the word *collogue*. The result is that the word *cóisireacht* 'gossiping' (appearing as 'cothering' and 'coshering') carries a pejorative meaning not usually present in the Irish word. While we can see how the act of gossiping could be viewed as negative, none of Ó Muirithe's citations carries that meaning. As only one Australian writer has used this word it is not easy to tell if the unusual meaning is the province of Charles De Boos's alone.

While there are far fewer nineteenth-century only words in the Australian Glossary compared with the Irish Glossary, their importance is increased if they have not been taken from literature, but rather from Irish English speech in Australia at the time. They offer an insight into the mindset and world view of the Irish as they settled into a new country. Such a mindset for many, if not the majority, of the Irish who migrated or were transported to Australia was influenced by the Catholic religion and later by the Famine. The word *scailp* and its diminutive form *scailpín*, it is a word particularly associated with the potato famine of the 1840s when many Irish people who had been evicted from their homes dug out crude shelters in ditches.[15] Only one writer in the Irish study wrote about the Famine, but it was the topic of choice for three Australian writers in the late twentieth century.

While the Australian writers' Irish characters seldom occupy centre stage, their depiction is no mere stereotype. Although many of the Irish words used as national markers are part of a standard vocabulary for both the Irish and Australian writer, there are sufficient divergences in the Australian usage to demonstrate an attempt to remain true to the type of Irish expression found in Australia. The language becomes a literary tool for the Australian writer, and we have seen that in recent times this awareness has increased. How the language is represented in writing is evidence of this new-found discovery.

The Written Representation of Irish: Spelling

The letters *j*, *k*, *q*, *v*, *w*, *x*, *y* and *z* are not native to the Irish language,[16] and occur only in loan words, usually those of a scientific or mathematical nature. Vowels in Irish are either short or long. A stroke or *síneadh fada* ('long lengthener' often spoken of as the simple *fada*) over the vowel indicates that it is long. Sometimes the presence of this stroke is all that separates one word from another; for example, the word *fear* 'man' becomes the word for 'grass' when a stroke is placed over the 'e': *féar*. Consonants in Irish are broad or slender. A consonant is broad or slender when it precedes or is followed by a broad vowel or slender vowel. Broad vowels are *a,o* and *u*, and slender vowels are *i* and *e*. The presence of a broad or slender vowel can affect pronunciation, as mentioned earlier with the case of *Sinn Féin*.[17] Another example is the word *girseach*, often rendered as *girsha*. The pronunciation of consonants can also change under the conditions of lenition and eclipsis. Lenition is indicated by placing 'h' after a consonant. For example, the word *cara* 'friend' undergoes lenition when preceded by the vocative particle: *a chara*. The pronunciation of the 'c' in *chara* is more guttural than in the word *cara*. Lenition in the case of the letter 'm' can produce a 'v' or 'w' sound as in the religious ejaculation *a Mhuire is Trua* where the *Mhuire* is pronounced 'wirreh'. Usually when 'm' is preceded or followed by a slender vowel it is pronounced 'v' as in the vocative phrase *a mhic* 'oh son' that is anglicised as 'avic'.

Eclipsis in Irish occurs when a consonant is placed in front of another consonant and the initial consonant is eclipsed, that is, it is no longer pronounced. An example is the word *páirc* 'field', that when preceded by the preposition *i* 'in', is written *i bpáirc* 'in a field' and only the 'b' is pronounced. In the same way the word *tír* 'country' is written *dtír* in the phrase *ár dtír* 'our country', and this affects the pronunciation as the 't' is no longer pronounced.

The long vowels a, o, and u, in the words *cáibín*, *bróg*, and *bastún*, and are conveyed in English writing as *caubeen*, *brogue* and *bostoon*. The vowels i and e in the words *bean sí* and *bréidín* are conveyed in the spelling *banshee* and *breadeen*. Vowel combinations in Irish such as *aoi* are pronounced 'ee' and usually anglicised as such, as in Australian examples already seen, *spraoi* as *spree* and *straoil* as *streel*.

Most of the Irish words used by Australian writers have been anglicised either because they are traditional words used in writing that features Irish characters, or they follow that pattern of anglicisation. A study of the history of anglicisation in Anglo-Irish writing has demonstrated a marked change in Irish writing from the 1950s and a return to orthodox spelling of even some of the most traditionally anglicised words.

Anglicisation

Most Irish words undergo anglicisation when they appear in print, and there are standard forms for many words. For example, the anglicisation of Irish words of endearment are regular, as indicated by this table.

Irish Spelling	Aust. Glossary	Irish Glossary	Ó Muirithe
a chara	A chara	acara	ahorra, achora
a chuisle mo chuisle	acushla, macush	acushla	acushla macushla
a chroí	achree,	achroidhe	a cree achree
a leanbh	alanna, alannah	alanna, alannah	alanna, alanah
a stór	astore, ashthore	asthore	asthore

The Australian spelling differs significantly in two words; *macush* and *ashthore*. The word *macush* is an abbreviation of anglicised *macushla* (Irish *mo chuisle*). This abbreviated spelling may be representative of the Australian tendency to shorten words. The spelling *ashthore* in the Australian Glossary appears to be an attempt to convey the Irish tendency to pronounce 's' as 'sh'. This occurs in Irish when 's' proceeds or is followed by a slender vowel; for example, *Síle* or *seamróg* (shamrock). In the Irish word *stór* 's' is followed by a broad vowel and so the pronunciation is 'store'. The Australian spelling *ashthore* is not the traditional anglicised form of *a stór*, and is an embellishment peculiar to the author Mary Fortune. Its context in *The Fortunes of Mary Fortune* is the sentence 'Oych! come in at wance, ashthore.' (65) where we can see that the spelling of English words has also been distorted for the purpose of conveying a strong dialectal accent. Elsewhere Fortune uses the standard form of *asthore*, so the form *ashthore* could also simply be a misspelling. Irish language terms of abuse are also retained in the English of Ireland and used by both Irish and Australian writers. This table demonstrates that there is general conformity in the anglicised spelling for *gaimbín* and *straoil* and significant spelling variations for the anglicisation of *amadán* and *spailpín*.

Irish Spelling	Aust. Glossary	Irish Glossary	Ó Muirithe
amadán	omadhaun omethaun omathaun	omadhaun omadhawn amadan	omadhaun omadhawn omadaun
gaimbín	gombeen	gombeen	gombeen
spailpín	spalpeen, spawlpeen shpalpeen, spilpeen	spalpeen	spawlpeen spalpeen
straoil	sthreel, streel	sthreel,streel	streel

These significant deviations in spelling for *amadán* and *spailpín* may indicate real life pronunciations. While the Irish Glossary and Ó Muirithe's spellings for *amadán* reflect the Irish language pronunciation, the Australian spellings of *omethaun* and *omathuan* would appear to indicate attempts to imitate the Australian pronunciation of the word. This pronunciation may have changed over time and developed the middle 't' sound.

Correct Spelling

My study of Irish language words in Anglo-Irish writing showed a marked de-anglicisation from the middle of the twentieth century in favour of a return to correct spelling of many words. I concluded that this was the result of the Irish education system that introduced the reading and writing of Irish to schoolchildren at the same time as that of English, around five years of age. The Irish reader is familiar with the look of an Irish word and its corresponding sound, so there is no need to anglicise its spelling. For example a word such as *amadán* 'fool' has been traditionally anglicised as *omadhaun*, but is written as *amadan* by Irish writers writing in the last half of the twentieth century. In the same way the word *oinseach* 'a foolish woman' is written as *oonshugh* in the nineteenth century but as *oinseach* in the twentieth century. Changes in the spelling of Irish words in Australian writing have also occurred between the nineteenth and twentieth centuries; however, these changes seem more to reflect the particular interest of an individual author than a change in the readership. The table below outlines Irish words correctly spelt in Australian writing.

Word	Anglicised form	Australian – time span	
bhrón (mo)	mavrone	1945 mavrone	1999 mo bhrón
cál ceannan	colcannon	1916 colcannon	1999 cál ceannan
poitín	poteen	1900–2001 poteen	1999/2002 poitín
sagart	soggarth	1919, 1973 soggarth	1998 sagart
scailpín	scalpeen	1998, 1999 scalpeen	1999 scailpeen

Christopher Koch spells all Irish words correctly in *Out of Ireland* (1999) because his characters are Irish speakers. Jill Blee has a heightened awareness of the Irish language and renders the word *poitín* correctly. In the Irish study only one writer was found who had made any changes to this long-term anglicised word. Australian Jill Blee retains the anglicised suffix 'een' in her spelling of *scailpín* as *scailpeen*. The Irish Australian writer, Kerry Murphy, uses the correct spelling of *sagart* because as an Irish speaker this form is more familiar to him than the anglicised one.

Glossing

Glossing of Irish language words in nineteenth century English texts is a common feature. Its purpose is both to provide an explanation for what may be a strange word to the average reader, and to convey the author's inside knowledge of this speech community or of language in general. Glossing may form part of the overall purpose of a book to inform the reader of something new. In my study of Irish words in Anglo-Irish writing I found that most of the nineteenth-century novels studied included glossing, although none explained all Irish words. This study, however, has found very little glossing in the nineteenth-century Australian writing examined.

The 'something new' in nineteenth-century Australian writing is Australia itself. When a nineteenth-century Australian writer does take time out to explain an Irish word, it may be reflective of their own particular interest rather than a concern for explanation itself. For example, in *Life in Victoria*, William Kelly glosses *caubeen* and *clauber* but not *arrah*, *brogues*, *faugh-a-ballagh*, *shillelagh* or *spalpeen*. This book is an account of the author's travels in Australia. Eight years before *Life in Victoria* Kelly's adventures in California were published. Kelly's readership for *Life in Victoria* was likely to be the practised or armchair traveller. William Kelly was born in Sligo and lived there until he was thirty. The unglossed words in *Life in Victoria* are not only well known Irish words in writing in English, but also part of Irish English. As a result of his upbringing in Ireland, Kelly may not have thought these words particularly strange. Kelly's glossing of *caubeen* is probably his or his editor's explanation for the choice of this word to describe the hat that the nineteenth-century London comic figure, Billy Barlow, would wear. The context is Kelly's description of a rough ride in a coach in Victoria when one passenger's head was driven through the roof after a particularly severe jolt:

> which produced instantaneous concussion of the hat, and presented one of the most ludicrous spectacles I ever beheld, like a man in a pillory crowned with the dilapidated caubeen of Billy Barlow.

The word *caubeen* is glossed as: 'Caubeen in Ireland is understood to mean a smashed hat'. Another word glossed in *Life in Victoria* is *clauber*. While Kelly, as an Irishman living in Sligo, may have come across Irish words, the word *clábar* 'mud' may not have been one of them; his social standing, perhaps, ensuring that it would not be part of the Irish English he would have been familiar with.

The glossing of *Anamondyoul* in Alexander Harris's *The Emigrant Family* as 'Obscure; presumably a phonetic spelling of a corrupt pronunciation' is significant, because it is the editor's gloss: the editor of the 1967 edition was

W.S.R. Ramson, then editor of *The Australian National Dictionary*. He did not recognise *Anamondyoul* as being a phonetic spelling of the Irish phrase *d'anam 'on diabhal* 'your soul to the devil'. Alexander Harris, however, made it clear in the novel that this was a common phrase: 'she merely uttered the regulation "Anamondyoul!" '. The speaker is 'Biddy', an Irish servant.

The glossing of *gassoon* and *spalpeen* for Ellen Davitt's nineteenth-century work *Force and Fraud* was part of the 1993 publication of the work; the first time the work had appeared as a novel. The publication of the text of *Force and Fraud* was part of the Mulini Press's series of nineteenth-century Australian writing appearing in print for the first time. As such the educating of the readership through the provision of a glossary is part of the awareness-raising process of a part of Australian history, rather than the nineteenth-century stance of author as educator. The editor of *Force and Fraud* glosses *gassoon* as:

> **gossoon** Anglo-Irish word derived from French garçon, describing a serving boy, lackey, or silly awkward fellow

and the word *spalpeen* is glossed as: 'from the Gaelic'. This is odd, as we do not say the word *frippery* is 'from the French' or that it is Anglo-French. We say it is 'French'. These Irish words in *Force and Fraud* are spelt according to English phonetics, but they are nonetheless Irish words and should be described as such.

Glossing of Irish words may also be a way of bringing knowledge of the Irish language to a readership that would appreciate such knowledge. Two works that provide significant glossing in this study were written in the twentieth century and for a predominantly Irish-background readership. Irish Australian priest and poet John O'Brien's *Around the Boree Log* was published in 1921. O'Brien had ministered to rural Irish communities in Australia. His book of Irish Australian poetry was well received in Australia and in Canada. William Carty's, *The Waves of Cool-a-vin*, was published in 1945. Carty was a fluent Irish speaker. The extensive glossing provided for Irish words in these two works may have been for the purpose of instructing an Irish diasporic readership in an aspect of their culture that they may not have had access to.

John O'Brien glosses all Irish words except for *achushla, alannah, boreen, colleen, keerschuch, gossoon, spleodar, spree,* and *shamrock*. Most of these are part of the standard vocabulary of Irish words used in English writing. O'Brien's readership was the Irish Catholic community in Australia and, as it turned out, throughout the world. Most of these words would therefore be familiar words in that speech community. The words *keerschuch* and *splather* were not glossed, perhaps because O'Brien did not know their Irish forms *céirseach* and *spleodar*.

William Carty glosses all Irish words except for *mavrone* and *wirristrue*. Carty's extensive glossing points to a desire to engage a readership that may be interested in his poetry but unfamiliar with Irish language words. Had Carty's book of poetry in English, *The Waves of Cool-a-vin*, been published in Ireland, the extensive glossing might not have occurred. The glossing of words in poetic works can have an adverse effect on the appearance of the poem on the page. Carty clearly wishes to instruct the reader on aspects of Irish culture that would not be generally known in Australia, but which are important to him. The exclamations *mavrone* and *wirristrue*, it could be argued, do not need explaining because they are followed by exclamation marks. Carty does, however, provide glosses for the exclamations *Aililiu* and *foirir*, because these exclamations are not usually part of the lexicon of writing in English.

Kerry Murphy in *Kerry Murphy's Memoirs* does not employ glossing, but rather explains unusual words within their context, such as the word *sool*. He explains:

> We fished for trout with a rod and what we called a 'sool' or eye, a little noose from a cow's tail.

Murphy uses another unusual Irish word in the lexicon of words used in writing in English: *croosted*, which he explains in context: 'and it was often we who croosted (threw) a few sods of keerans at him'. I have not been able to find the word *keerans* under its probable spelling of *ciarán* in any of the Irish language dictionaries. It is likely to be a word specific to Murphy's homeland that has not been captured in print until this Australian publication. Murphy writes for an Irish-born readership in Australia that shares his background. For this readership he provides Irish language phrases that are not explained, such as *Ni Bheidh A Leitheid Ann Go Deo* and *Buidhcheas le Dia*. For the readers who share his sporting interest he can use the specific hurling term *to puck out*. Another readership Murphy appears to keep in mind is the Australian community he has lived among. Most Irish-born people would know the word *Feis*. Murphy explains: 'Today there are music festivals or *Feiseanna* all over Ireland'.

Christopher Koch provides a glossary under the title 'Editor's Notes' at the end of *Out of Ireland*, in which all Irish words and phrases are explained. This is in keeping with the nineteenth-century subject matter and style he has adopted; the editor is a fictitious character in the 'found document'. Overall, in twentieth-century Australian writing, if an explanation is given to an Irish language word it is more than likely to occur in the body of the text either in the dialogue or by way of an authorial comment. For instance Jill Blee's *Brigid* (1999) explains the word *bóithrín* through dialogue:

> What's here? I can't see anything ...
> *The boithrín, the bóithrín. Go down the bóithrín*
> I don't know what a boreen is. There's nothing here but fields.
> *The opening in the hedge. The bóithrín, the lane.* (44)

Blee also draws attention to the Irish language word *bóithrín* by including the more recognisable anglicised word *boreen*. This is in keeping with Blee's own awareness of the Irish language. *Brigid* is 'faction', a true account with fictional elements of an Australian (Blee) visiting Ireland to search for her ancestor's homeland. The narrator of the novel says at one point:

> It hadn't occurred to me that English wasn't the spoken language here and that my great grandfather, far from being a Gaelic scholar as my mother had claimed, simply continued to speak his native tongue at every opportunity. (113)

This was also Jill Blee's personal opinion while writing this novel. According to family lore, her ancestor taught the Irish language in Ballarat, Victoria.

While the author as educator is no longer a stance taken by twentieth-century writers, these Australian writings with an Irish focus use glossing and explication within the text to emphasise the Irish language as well as to provide meaning to words. Their own interest in and value of the language is what separates them from other Australian writers who use Irish words but do not explain them, or explain them only through the filter of English. This awareness-raising of the Irish language in twentieth-century Australian writing is notable. It may represent a growing awareness of languages other than English, as a result of the focus on multiculturalism. It may also represent an increase in knowledge of the Irish language as a result of technology and low-cost travel. Most importantly, perhaps, the Irish language is one area of Irish Australian culture that is not tainted with the convict or low-class historical stain. The emphasis of Irish words through italicisation is another form of elevating and drawing attention to the language.

Italicisation

The Irish study found that most nineteenth-century works presented Irish words in italics or inverted commas, although this did not apply to all words. It found that in twentieth-century Irish writing the trend was to present Irish words as part of English expression in Ireland, although the return to correct Irish orthography meant that these words did not look like English words. The study concluded that the non highlighting of Irish words in English language writing in the second half of the twentieth century demonstrated an unconscious form of code switching in the ease with which Irish words have been integrated into English in Ireland.

A program commemorating the visit to Sydney of Irish Prime Minister Eamon de Valera in 1948. The slogan at the bottom says 'God Free Ireland!'. (The name at the top is the National Irish Association, who sponsored the visit.) de Valera spoke in Irish at the meetings he attended to gain support for a free Ireland. In 1949 his government declared Ireland a republic.

The highlighting of Irish words in Australian writing through italicisation or the use of inverted commas is relatively rare before the 1980s. In addition, only two words, *dúidín* and *fáilte* are highlighted in nineteenth-century literature. The highlighting of Irish words in Australian writing occurs for two reasons: (1) to indicate that the Irish language is being spoken, and (2) to indicate a formal, traditional and historical form of a word. The latter is apparent in the highlighting of the word *dúidín* ('a short pipe', as *doodeen*).

An introductory course designed by the author for Australian students

This word is not glossed, however, by any of the writers and it has not been included in Australian dictionaries. The word is in the 'reject' files at the Australian National Dictionary Centre, a place where words are kept that may be relevant, but in the end do not make the final cut for inclusion in the dictionary. The result is that this Irish word has not been credited publicly with playing the significant part it did in the description of the look of the colonial male and female of the lower classes. The word *fáilte* 'welcome' is used in the phrase *céad míle fáilte,* a traditional Irish greeting of welcome meaning 'a hundred thousand welcomes' and so its appearance in print is usually indicative of the most traditional of Irish settings or one in which this Irish language phrase was a natural part of speech. The word or phrase may be the only Irish language expression heard in that setting, but the highlighting of it indicates that it stands for the whole language. For example, in Tim Winton's *The Riders* the Australian visitor is introduced to the language through being taught the traditional way of saying a toast: 'Cheers! Slainte'.

Of the Australian authors studied Christopher Koch and Jill Blee make extensive use of highlighting for their Irish language words and phrasing, and, as was discussed under the section on 'spelling' they use Irish orthography in the depiction of Irish words. Elsewhere, words that are highlighted to draw attention to their role as cultural and historical items include: *aisling*, italicised by Miles Franklin and Christopher Koch; *vanithee* (pronunciation of Irish *bean tí*) in Thomas Keneally's *The Great Shame*; and *craic,* 'fun', and *Fleadh Ceol* by Kerry Murphy in his memoirs. As most of the italicised Irish words in Australian writing occur in works written in the 1990s we may be seeing the effects of improved technology where the method for italicisation and indicating the Irish mark of vowel lengthening (the *fada*) is part of the average word-processor.

The decision to highlight an Irish language word in print in Australian writing is not subject to the same historical influences that appear to have influenced Irish writing. The conscious highlighting of Irish language words in Australian writing brings an added value to Irish Australian subject material. It implies that the writer has expert knowledge of a rare item and so increases that writer's value in the Australian market. It also demonstrates proper recognition of the Irish language as a relevant and functioning language, and so increases the Australian writer's chance of increasing an Irish market for their work.

Notes

1 Dymphna Lonergan, 'The Significance of Irish Gaelic in Anglo-Irish Writing 1800–1989', MA Thesis, Flinders University of South Australia 1994. 140–167.

2 James M. Clark, *The Vocabulary of Anglo-Irish*, St Gall: Folcroft Library Editions, 1974. 31–32.

3 Con Costello, *Botany Bay*. 98.

4 Patrick Farrell, *The Irish in Australia* (1987). 55–56.

5 Marion Miller Knowles, *Pierce O'Grady's Daughter*, Sydney: Pellegrini Co., 1926. 184–85.

6 'The Significance of Irish Gaelic in Anglo-Irish Writing 1800–1989'. 77.

7 G.L. Brook, *Varieties of English*, London: Macmillan, 1973. 39.

8 Christy Brown, *Down All the Days*, London: World Books, 1971. 59.

9 *The Irish in Australia* (1987). 17.

10 K.H. Connell, *Irish Peasant Society*, Dublin: Irish Academic Press, 1996. 18.

11 William Howitt, *Land, Labour and Gold*, Kilmore: Lowden Publishing Company, 1972.

12 Patrick O'Farrell, *The Irish in Australia* (1987). 106.

13 ibid. 107.

14 ibid. 269.

15 I have been informed that in the mining district of Kapunda in South Australia where there was a large force of Irish labourers in the 1850s, there are the remains of crude shelters dug out of the hillsides.

16 The following discussion on the nature of Irish spelling uses much of the section on spelling that precedes the Glossary in my study 'The Significance of the Irish Language in Anglo-Irish Writing 1800–1989'.

17 I use this term for explication of a spelling rule because it is one that is familiar to many people. Elsewhere in this discussion I will use words from the Glossary, where possible.

Chapter Five

Smidiríní

Fragments

While undergoing assimilation, generations of Irish Australians have kept an anxious eye on Ireland's political struggles. Irish Australian newspapers were a source of such information as Irish affairs were significant features up until the 1920s and Home Rule. Through snippets such as advertisements, letters to the editor, poems and general articles, we can see a clear connection between the Irish language and Irish politics. In particular, at times of crisis or high significance, such as the struggle for Home Rule and anniversaries of political uprisings, the Irish in Australia often turned to their native language to express what could not be expressed in English. At other times we can see the promotion of Irish for its linguistic and cultural sake. Indeed, promoters of the Irish language in Australia were often Australian-born and had developed an interest in the language in Australia. This section, *Smidiríní* (the Irish word is the origin of English *smithereens*), provides a necessarily brief insight into the Irish language as it appears in some Irish Australian newspapers.

Also included in this section are samples of poetry written in Irish by three Irish-born poets who spent some time in Australia, and an extract from Australian Vincent Buckley's poem 'Gaeltacht', written during one of his many sojourns in Ireland.

During my search, I was delighted to come across a Queensland poet, William Carty, who not only wrote poetry that was speckled with Irish language words, but also a volume of Irish language poetry, under the name Fionán Mac Cártha, that was published after his death in 1953.

Fionán Mac Cártha was born in Roscommon in the west of Ireland in 1886. As a young man he took an interest in the Irish language. Self-taught, he gained fluency in Irish through conversing with the old people in the district and attendance at language schools.[1] As a twenty-year-old, he was a

William Carty wrote Irish language poems in Queensland under his Irish name, Fionán Mac Cártha.
PHOTO COURTESY OF *TÁIN*

member of *Conradh na Gaeilge*, the Gaelic League, an organisation that was founded in 1893 with the purpose of maintaining spoken Irish in Ireland. One of the manifestations of the League's work was the annual *Oireachtas;* an Arts Festival conducted in the Irish language. At the 1907 *Oireachtas* Mac Cártha was hailed as 'a new voice in Ireland' in response to his 'Ode of Welcome' to Dr Douglas Hyde, the President of the Gaelic League and later first President of Éire, the Irish Free State. In 1913 Hyde provided a written reference for Mac Cártha saying that he was

> An accomplished poet, to my mind One of the best Irish poets in Ireland today.

Hyde also wrote the Foreword to *The Waves of Cool-a-vin,* a collection of poetry written during Mac Cártha's years in Australia. In this section I have provided the poems 'Aililiu' and 'Lá in Astraoile' ('a day in Australia') as examples of Mac Cártha's English and Irish language poetry.

For a short time in the 1980s and '90s Melbourne was home to Irish-born poet Louis de Paor. de Paor was born in Cork in 1961 and immigrated to Australia in 1987. He spent six years in Melbourne before returning to live in Ireland. Some of his poetry from his time in Australia was published in Melbourne. The collection *Aimsir Bhreicneach/Freckled Weather* was shortlisted in Australia for the Dinny O'Hearn/SBS Bookshow Award for Literary translations in 1994. His second collection of poetry, *Gobán Cré is Cloch/Sentences of Earth and Stone,* was funded in part by the Literature Board of Australia and Arts and Writers' organisations in Tasmania. Louis de Paor's brief residence in Australia was influential in the role he played in the multicultural life of the country. He was involved in the setting up of the first Irish community radio program in Melbourne. He also conducted Irish language lessons for the Irish Australian community there. Apart from the two collections of poetry that were published in Australia, de Paor's poetry also appeared in Australian literary outlets such as *Meanjin* and *Australian Short Stories*. In the Preface to *Aimsir Bhreicneach/Freckled Weather*, Helen Fulton from the Centre for Celtic Studies at the University of Sydney said that de Paor's work is important because it contributes to the rich multicultural fabric that is Australia:

> The work of Louis de Paor is part of that richness, articulating for us an experience of humanity that challenges the imperialism of language and crosses the boundaries of difference.

In both collections the English and Irish versions of the poems are placed on opposite pages. Helen Fulton claims that through this device the English language is no longer the dominant language. For those who know the Irish language it is clear that the English in de Paor's collections is not a translation of the Irish, nor is the Irish that of the English. His long poem about Irish convicts buried in Australia, 'The Isle of the Dead' or *Oileán na Marbh*, demonstrates this.

Finally, the poem 'Cian' by Kerry-Gaeltacht born Eilín Ní Bheaglaoich offers a different perspective on the Irish migrant experience; in this poem the poet's Australian born son, Cian, is lamenting the loss of his Australian home as a result of the family decision to move to Ireland. This poem appears in *The Turning Wave*, a comprehensive collection of over two hundred years of Irish Australian songs and poems.

These *smidiríní* and the chapters in this book point to the many areas in which the Irish in Australia have sounded their thoughts and feelings, hopes and dreams for centuries.

A contemporary CD by Melbourne-based native Irish speaker Muiris (Mossie) Ó Scanláin featuring songs in Irish and Australian, and paying homage to two 'home' countries.

The Exile of Erin

There came to the beach a poor Exile of Erin;
The dew on his thin robe was heavy and chill;
For his country he sigh'd, when at twilight repairing,
To wander alone by the wind-beaten hill.
But the day-star attracted his eyes sad devotion;
For it rose o'er his own native isle of the ocean,
Where once in the fire of his youthful emotion,
He sung the bold anthem of Erin-go-Bragh.

(*The Irish Exile: Freedom's Advocate* (Hobart),
26 January, 1850, p. 7)

Untitled

When I sailed from the land that was dear to my youth,
I might ask of my heart how it fares;
I could question my soul if its pillow was smooth,
Or its mind were unraised with cares.

But my heart's hopeless care, and my sad soul could say,
That their inward affections were sore.
Ah, but wild was my grief, when I hastened away,
And banished from Erin ma Store.

(*The Irish Exile: Freedom's Advocate* (Hobart), 8 June, 1850, p. 4)

The Irish-Australian

Australia is my place of birth,
I love this land it's true,
And I love the land my father loved,
My mother loved it too.
They call it Erin's sainted isle,
The fairest spot on earth,
I love it, yes, why should I not?
It gave my parents birth.

In the days so long ago,
When I was very young,
My father taught me on his knee
To speak the Irish tongue.
Though dead for years (God rest his soul),
I still remember well,
And retain until the day I die
The tales he used to tell.

I have books my mother used to read-
They tell of Ireland's wrongs,
And others bound in green and gold,
Inspiring poems and songs.
They tell sad tales of evil days,
When the tyrant's scourging hand
Forced her son to seek a home
In some far distant land.

Providence may yet prove unkind,
If fortune smiles on me,
I'll take a trip to Erin's Isle,
Across the deep blue sea.
Men may scoff at Ireland's brogue,
They may all say what they will,
I can love Australia's sunny land,
And love old Ireland still.

(*The Irish Australian* (Sydney)
October 13, 1894, p. 8)

The Irish Language

To The Editor

Sir?

It may be of interest to some of your readers to know that the movement for the preservation of the Irish language promises to be very successful. Besides the excellent monthly, the *Gaelic Journal*, now in its eighth yearly volume, published by the Gaelic League at 4d. a number in Dublin, partly in English and partly in Irish, and which numbers amongst its subscribers several persons in this province, including the Public Library Board which takes the handsome yearly volume, there was started on the 8th January a weekly called 'Fáinne an Lae' (Dawn of Day) of which four numbers have reached me. This weekly is published at one penny by Mr Bernard Doyle, of Upper Ormond Quay, Dublin. The fourth number contains many locals relating to Ireland, news from over the sea (Tar Saile), a London letter and news, church information (all in Irish), Gaelic doings (Gnóta na Gaedilge), and a lengthy and very favorable review from the London Athenaum, a paper by the late Thos. Davis on 'National Language', and other items of interest. It mentions also that the 'Star', a London evening paper, published a notice of 'Fáinne an Lae' both in Irish and English before some of the Dublin evening papers.

I am, Sir &c.,
Chas. T. Hargrave.
Kent Terrace, Norwood,
March 1, 1898

(*Southern Cross* (Adelaide) 4 March, 1898, p. 3)

In Memoriam[2]
'My dark Shauneen'

(Expressive of the anxiety of an Irish Australian mother for her son at the front)

My dark Shauneen to war has gone,
Mo Shauneen dhuv, mo Shaun.
Oh, bright the light that led him on,
Mo Shauneen dhuv, mo Shaun!
'Speed, O youth,' the beacon cried,
'Thy barque across the ocean tide.'
And Freedom now shall be his guide
Mo Shauneen dhuv, mo Shaun!

Your arm is strong, your cause is right,
Mo Shauneen dhuv, mo Shaun!
And as you strike, your spirit's light,
Mo Shauneen dhuv, mo Shaun!
But who can know, brave Faly's son,
The sad tears from my eyes that run,
While seas divide and I'm alone,
Mo Shauneen dhuv, mo Shaun!

(Added on learning that her son had been killed in action)

The Wall has echoed 'mid the night!
Mo Shauneen dhuv, mo Shaun!
Oh, gone for aye my soul's delight,
Mo Shauneen dhuv, mo Shaun!
No earthly joy may now be mine,
Since I to tears must e'er incline–
To think a distant grave is thine,
Mo Shauneen dhuv, mo Shaun!
God rest you, then, mo boucaleen,
Mo Shauneen dhuv, mo Shaun!

(*The Advocate* (Melbourne) 16 September, 1916, p. 16)

A Chuthaigh Mhalluigthe[3]

A chuthaigh mhalluigthe ár is easgaine ort
agus gráin Mhic Dé,
agus ar an ngasraidh do bhí ceangailte go
dlúth id' thaobh,
do dhearbhuigh i láthair Sasannach ar an
dtriúr i mbréig,
do chuir na farairí thar na farrgí go dtí
na New South Wales.

Tá an chroc na seasamh 's an chnáib dá casadh
dúinn leath bhliadhain roimh-ré,
go ndeaghaidh na dearbhuigthe isteach a gan
fhios dúinn ag an dream gan séan,
mura mbeadh feabhas ar gcarad go mbeadh
ár muinéil cnagtha go doirnín gan aol,
chum gur casadh sinn chum ár dtearma chai-
theamh in na New South Wales.

You Furious One Accursed

You furious one accursed! Plague and
Malediction on you! and the disgust of God's Son!
and on the band connected closely with you,
who swore falsely against the three in
the presence of the English.
And who sent the heroes over the
ocean to New South Wales.

The gallows is reared and the hemp is twisted
twisted for the half a year beforehand,
and the oaths were admitted unknown
to us by the unholy gang;
Only for the worth of our friends our
necks would have been cracked and
deep in the lime,
but instead we were fated to spend our
term in New South Wales.

(*The Advocate* (Melbourne) 17 March 1917, p. 11)

Norah O'Neill

That Norah O'Neill is a sthreel,
And I'm talking the way that I feel,
With her dowdy old hat, and her hair pasted flat,
And her skirt bobbing after her heel;
And there to the church she will steal,
And under the lamp she will kneel
When confessions are done, and there's never a one
To be heard but that Norah O'Neill.

It annoys the priest's man a great deal,
And it makes every one boogathiel
At him scraping the floor, yes, and rattlin' the door
Just to hurry my lady O'Neill.
But there she will squat on her heel,
While over the forms he will steal;
He would put out the light and close up for the night?
But he can't for that keershuch O'Neill.

I believe (and I talk as I feel
When there at the Judgment we kneel,
And, each in his place, is the whole human race?
One half to be sent to the deil?
That, just as they're setting the seal,
A dust-cloud a glance will reveal
At the end of the day, Jerusalem way;
And you'll find 'twill be Norah O'Neill,
with her skirt bobbing after her heel,
And we'll have to go through the whole business anew;
Och, Norah O'Neill is a sthreel.

('John O'Brien' *Around the Boree Log,*
Sydney: Angus and Robertson, 1921, p. 96)

Michael O'Keefe – Irish Lexicographer: The Man and His Work

Michael O'Keefe, now living in Bankstown, Sydney, was born near Miltown Malbay, Co. Clare about seventy years ago. At that time the place was an Irish-speaking district. Today the Gaelic tongue is little spoken there, but a rich Gaelic tradition still survives in it. After leaving school Mr. O'Keefe became a sculptor, a trade which he subsequently abandoned for the teaching profession. Later in life he entered the Civil Service, from which he afterwards resigned, and came to Australia. How he came to interest himself in Irish lexicography and became the author of Australia's first contribution to Gaelic studies is known to very few and, will, undoubtedly interest readers of *The Gael*. It happened thus. Some years ago a man named Eugene Ryan[4] conducted a private school in the vicinity of St. Benedict's Church, Sydney, and amongst the subjects which he taught was the Irish language. Gaelic text-books were then difficult to procure, and Gaelic dictionaries were wholly unobtainable. At the request of the headmaster Mr. O'Keefe compiled a miniature Irish dictionary for the use of the pupils in the Gaelic class. Taking a fancy to the work, he decided to write a complete Gaelic dictionary, a work which took him many years to accomplish. He was severely handicapped in his task as he had no Irish scholars to consult, no Gaelic books for reference and no sympathetic fellow-countrymen to encourage him. Nevertheless he succeeded in producing a work unsurpassed by anything in Irish lexicography, except the monumental dictionary of Fr. Dineen, published last year by the Irish Text's Society of London. Mr O'Keefe brought his work under the notice of several prominent Irishmen in Australia with the view of enlisting their support for its publication, but without success. There were three amongst them, however, who displayed a keen interest in it: His Eminence, the late Patrick Francis Cardinal Moran, Rev. T.A. Fitzgerald, O.F.M., the well-known Irish writer, and Mr. Tighe Ryan, late editor of the *Catholic Press*. When the present writer arrived in Australia Mr. O'Keefe's manuscript was in the possession of Father Fitzgerald. After the death of this renowned Franciscan priest, the writer became acquainted with Mr. O'Keefe through the agency of Mr. Tighe Ryan, and secured the manuscript, which he sent by Sir Hubert Murray, Governor-General of British New Guinea, to the Dublin Gaelic League for examination. The experts of the Gaelic League in Dublin passed it for publication, and subsequently a committee was formed in Sydney to raise funds for putting Australia's first contribution to Gaelic studies in the hands of the public … Soon after the first meeting of the publication committee a communication was received from Dublin intimating that part of the manuscript had mysteriously disappeared. The author was informed, and immediately supplied the missing part. which was sent to the Gaelic League without delay. The complete manuscript is now in the hands of Mr. Frank Fahy, B.A. late secretary of the Irish Gaelic League, who with Miss B.J. MacGarry, late secretary of *The Gael* has been commissioned to look after its interests in Ireland. Arrangements have been practically completed with a certain publishing house in Dublin to produce the book, and the road is now clear for the publication committee in Australia to begin its work.[5]

The Gael (Sydney) Vol. 7 no. 5 August, 1929, pp.10–11

Aililiu

Aililiu! But it's lonely,
Alone in this lonesome place,
Aililiu! But it's lonely,
With the cold death, face to face;
Aililiu! But it's lifeless,
Though alive, there's no life in me,
I am far away from the Old Land,
And my own folks o'er the sea.

O some make money their measure,
Pleasure, or place or power,
But give me health and the love of friends,
And a book for the quiet hour;
And some love the crowded places
Where the birds and flowers are few;
Give me the road and the open air,
And the green hills, and the blue.

O the Being that wove the beauty
Of earth and the heaven above,
Who made the lion and the lamb,
The serpent and the dove,
Gave love to sweeten sorrow,
And sorrow to deepen love,
For the thyme is sweet, but sweeter,
When trodden, the scent thereof.

Och! It's not for death I'm caring
For the Lord will claim His own,
But to leave my bones among strangers
In a strange land all unknown.
O my ghost will walk the roadway
By the lone lake of Loch Glynn,
And the moonlight, like enchantment,
The cool, dark woods within.

(William Carty, *The Waves of Cool-a-vin*, Brisbane:
The Co-operative Press, 1945, p. 15)

Lá In Astraoile

Táim ag siubal ar árdán aoibhinn, is an ghrian gheal ag éirighe,
An drúcht glas a sméideadh ar an bhféar úr n-a luighe.
Coillte nár chuir duine thart timpeall, 's na sléibhte
Thar gualainn a chéile ag gobadh aníos.
Acht tá an saoghal ar fad uaigneach, agus m'intinn go buartha
Mé féin bheith le fada, fada i bhfad ó thír mo dhúthchais;
Go Luan a' lae bhráth, Luan nach dtiocfaidh go bráth,
Ní fheicfear scáil ann, i mbaile ná i dtír.

Ní cháinim Astraoile, tá sláinte na gcéadta
Le fagháil san aer glégeal, is sa' mbaladh ar an gcraoibh;
Lá geimhridh chó breágh le lá Beátain' i n-Éirinn
Acht mo bheannacht don Ghaedhealtacht ó's léi tá mo chroidhe.
Mé féachaint na sléibhte, 's mé cuimhniú ar Shligeach.
Nó 'g éisteacht na n-éanlaith, 's mo smaointe ar Loch Glinne;
Na beacha go beó 'déanamh meala agus ceóil?
Ach! Baile-na-móna, 's an bláth bán arís!

Céad slán le Loch Glinne na gcoillte glas aerach,
Mbíonn glonradh ón ngréin ann, agus dídean le fagháil,
An londubh 's an smól ag comórtas le chéile,
'S nach bródamhail, binn-bhréithreach an uiseóg go h-árd!
Galoidh na cuaiche go fuaim-bhinn ag tigheacht de bhárr géige,
Sluaighte sidhe fá na gleanntaibh, sluaighte aingeal ar aer ann;
'S níl pósaidh ná plannda, nach bhfásann I gcubhra
I ngáirdín na cúirte, cois balla nó i bplás.

(Fionán Mac Cártha, *Amhráin Ó Dheireadh an Domhan*,
Dublin: Oifig an tSoláthair, 1953, p. 48)

ST PATRICK'S DAY MESSAGE FROM PRESIDENT DE VALERA

To all our good friends beyond the seas, greetings and good wishes on this St Patrick's Day.

For generations St Patrick's Day has been set apart for the public acknowledgement of God's goodness to our people in enriching them with the treasures of St Patrick's faith and in sustaining them through centuries of trial and sorrow.

This year we are commemorating the fiftieth anniversary of the 1916 Uprising, that heroic deed from which has come freedom to the greater part of our country. On this St Patrick's Day, then, let us recall particularly the memory of those leaders and men who in the Uprising gave their lives for our country and let us renew our determination to play a full part in making Ireland the nation of their desire.

May God, through the intercession of St Patrick, bless the labours of all our kin and friends abroad and give them and the people among whom they dwell peace and happiness.

Ar choimrí Dé go raibh gach duine dár gcáirde agus sonas go dtuga Sá go fial dóibhshean agus dúinne in Éirinn.

~ EAMON DE VALERA

(*The Advocate* (Melbourne), 17 March 1966, p. 16)

Gaeltacht

Many Gaeltachts:
Spiral inside spiral
Worm in the apple.

Through the rain-shellacked glass
you keep looking for some way
into it, letting your mind bulb around one
image or another: Damp paddocksfull
of white refuse burning
near Milltown: At Dingle, among papier m?ché
cowboy hats, the butcher stooping
into his car's trunk for the carcasses:
Errigal the cone of buckled waste, its evening
Light spitting at your eyes
like boiling metal: and at
Meenlaragh the young girls flirting
disdainfully with old men.

Summer. The land
collapsing from one heat
to another, the bay
drained, brown with mud
under brown water thin
as a mirage. Yet, miles inland, as I
pulled the heather from the road's
rockface, I could feel the sea
penetrate my hand.

Autumn. A groincold shrinking
in the land itself: a stone country that never
comes to full colour, except in the knife-glint
of a wave: houses, stones laid inside stones,
believed in fearfully as holy wells.

(Vincent Buckley, *The Pattern*, Oxford:
Oxford University Press, 1979, p. 10)

'The Isle of the Dead' *Oileán na Marbh*

The headstones face home
to England where a world
is turning against the sun,
her colonies a fleet of
drifting stars follow the
glow of a fake lodestone,
lured by its deceiving light,

Tá aghaidh na leac
ó thuaidh ar Shasana
mar a gcasann domhan
ruathalach ar fhearsaid,
réaltaí timpeall ar
adhmaintchloch bhréige
á dtarraingt le neamhthoil
ag a loinnir chaoch

On the south side of
the island away from the
sea the convicts lie as
they did in life on edge
in cramped beds that hurled
them against walls or knocked
them to the floor if they
moved in their sleep

Ar an dtaobh theas
den oileán ón bhfarraige
luíonn na cimí mar
luíodar lena mbeo
ar thochtanna róchúng
a dhoirtfeadh le falla
nó amach ar urlár iad
dá mba chorrach a suan

If I call them out
the grass will not reveal
their names until the wind
bows the stunted trees as
they stand to attention and
from the deaf and dumb
cell of the earth a multitude
rises before the sun
straight and proud as
headstones, Thomas Kelly,
carpenter, Edwin Pinder,
miner, John Bowden, barber
James Parsons, sailor, Thomas Loague,
cobbler

Má ghoirim chugham iad
ní labharfaidh an fear
orthu le náire shaolta
nó go gcromann an ghaoth
muinéal mileata na gcrann
is plódaíonn aniar as balbh
chealla talaimh bhodhair
na sluaite ainm chomh
díreach le leac gan
chlaonadh, Thomas Kelly,
siúnéir, Edwin Pinder,
mianadóir, James Parsons,
mairnéalach, Tomás Loague,
gréasaí

a meitheal of labourers
Shovelling earth from their
Eternal dust, Terence
McMahon from County
Clare, John Arnold, Norbury,
John Healy, a Kerryman
and their comrades as yet
un-named, a roll-call,
unopened,
a snail's trail across
eternity, a shower of rain
without stain that bows
my head and inflexible
knee in supplication
to the earth.

meitheal
spailpín ag sluaistiú
scraith na síoraíochta
dá cgré, Terence McMahon
ó Chontae an Chláir,
John Arnold, Norbory Shasana,
John Healy, Ciarraíoch
gona mbráithre fós gan
scaoileadh, glae seilide
ar shlí na fírinne, baisteach
gan sal a umhlaíonn mo cheann
is mo ghlúin righin
is paidir chun talaimh.

(Louis de Paor, *Gobán Cré is Cloch/Sentences of Earth and Stone,* Melbourne: Black Pepper Press, 1996, pp. 6–21)

Cian[6]

Tréigfeadsa 'n t-imeall so thuas in uachtar
'S déanfad mo threoir ó dheas;
Gan mhairg a' t'aistear
Tré néalta lasrach fillfead ar Thír an Óir.

Scaras led chóstai buí coiréalach
Gan beann ar mhalairt spéire:
Cloisim trim neal do mheallach uaigneach
Mo thriall dtí 'd dhraíocht ó dheas.

Aithneod na fásaigh blabha
Monabhar rúnda laoi:
Buille arsa chorroboree
Cuisle na hoíche dhuibe.

Fillfeadsa fhéin ar thír thá lonrach,
Arbhar buí is fíon
Tabharfad mo chúl le sléibhte gorma
'S an fiolar ag éamh cois cuan.

Tréigfeadsa 'n t-imeall so thuas in uachtar
'S déanfad mo thoir ó dheas:
Gan mhairg a' t-a
Tré nélta lasrach fillfead ar Thír an Óir.

(*The Turning Wave: Poems and Songs of Irish Australia*,
Colleen Z. Burke and Vincent Woods eds,
Sydney: Kardoorair Press Pty Ltd, 2001, p. 256)

Prize-winning translation

In the first issue of Táin *we offered a prize for the best translation of Máire Mhac an tSaoi's Christmas poem. Thanks to those who sent in entries. Here is the poem with the prize-winning translation submitted by Áine Szymanski.*

Oíche Nollag

Le Máire Mhac an tSaoi

Le coinnle na n-aingeal tá spéir amuigh breactha,
Tá fiacail an tseaca sa ghaoith ón gcnoc,
Adaigh an tine is téir chun na leapan,
Luífidh Mac Dé ins an tigh seo anocht.
Fágaidh an doras ar leathadh ina coinne,
An nhaighdean a thiocfaidh is a naí ar a hucht,
Deonaigh do shuaimhneas a ligint, a Mhuire,
Luíodh Mac Dé ins an tigh seo anocht.
Bhí soilse ar lasadh I dtigh sin na haíochta,
Cóirú gan caoile, bia agus deoch,
Do ceannaithe olla, do ceannaithe síoda,
Ach luífidh Mac Dé ins an tigh seo anocht.

Christmas Night

The sky is speckled with the candles of angels,
There's a bit of frost in the wind from the hill,
Light the fire now and off to bed with you,
God's Son will sleep in this house tonight.
Leave the door ajar for them,
The young girls who will come nursing her infant.
Mary, take your ease and rest here,
Let God's Son lie in this house tonight.
The light is shining in this privileged house,
Everything is ready, food and drink,
We've bought oil and silk,
But God's Son will lie in this house tonight.

(*Táin* (Melbourne) March 2000, p. 37)

A story of the supernatural

Ni fhaca siad an tsamhail

Colin Ryan has adapted this story of the supernatural from the telling of Tadhg O Buachalla, An Tailliuir, who lived in West Cork.

Bhi fear i gCill Gharbhain. Sean O Conchuir ab ainm do. Bhiodh se ag imeacht i dteannta na bpncai.

Bhi fear eile, Sean O Suibhne, ar na Stiallachaibh (1). Bhi inion ag Sean O Suibhne. Wire ab ainm di. Dar Dia, buaileadh an inion breoite, agus bhi siad craite ciapaithe aici. Ni raibh si ag dul i bhfeabhas, agus ni raibh si ag dul in olcas. Sa deireadh chuaigh Sean ag triall ar Shean O Conchuir. Bhi se raite go mbiodh se siud i dteannta na bpucai agus go raibh fios gach ni aige.
Bhi an t-athair ag deanamh amach (2) narbh i a inion a bhi ann in aon chor ach gur rug na pucai leo i agus gur chuir siad samhail (3) ina hion-ad. Ni reiteodh fuar na te, dubh na geal, lei. D'inis se an sceal do Shean O Conchtiir.

'O, td si imithe,' a duirt Sean O Conchuir. 'Mo chomhairle duitse anois gan aon droch-chor a thabhairt di seo, mar an cor a gheobhaidh si uait gheobhaidh d'inion an cor ceanna uathu sin. Td an abhainn congarach duit. T6g amach i sin agus caith isteach san abhainn i. Mura snamhfaidh si anonn trasna na habhann b'fhearr duit i a shabhail. Ach dean-faidh; snamhfaidh si.'

D'imigh Sean abhaile. Thog se leis amach an tsamhail seo a bhi sa leaba agus chaith isteach san abhainn i. D'imigh si anonn go dti an taobh eile den abhainn. Thainig a chailin fein on taobh eile den abhainn ansin. Bhi si chomh maith agus a bhi si riamh, ach ni neosfadh si (4) pioc doibh. Ni fhaca siad an tsamhail as sin amach, na nior togadh an cailin uathu.

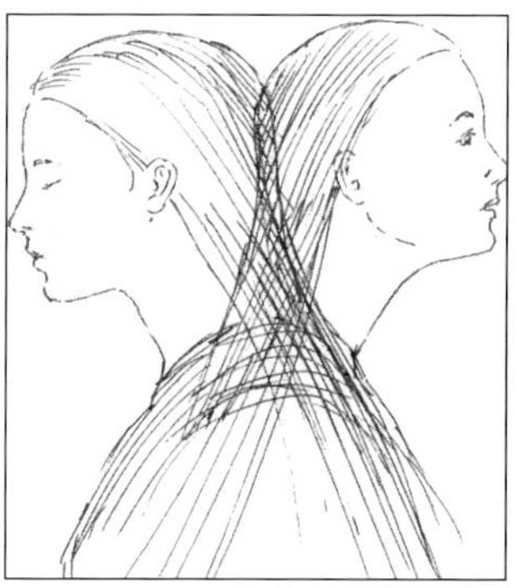

Reprinted from *TAIN*, April-May 2001

Notes

1 All biographical information has been taken from Gregory Byrne's conference paper '"Exile From Home":The Poems of Fionán Mac Cártha, 1886-1953' in *Éire*-Ireland, Summer 1995. 118–130.

2 Corporal Jaguers was the son of the acting-president of the United Irish League of Victoria, and he was also secretary of the Young Ireland Society in Melbourne. The report of Jaguers' death covers one quarter of the page. The heading in Gothic type reads: 'Corporal John Davitt Jaguers/Killed in Action in France'. Jaguers is described as 'an active, high-spirited, muscular youth, well over six feet in height … but slightly over 21 years'. He had been injured at Lone Pine and declined 'the opportunity to return to Australia and a clerical position, opting instead to return to serve with his old battalion that had moved on to France'.

3 The poem appears in Gaelic font. The *Advocate* purchased the 'new fount of Gaelic type in 1902 and used it to print Irish language lessons and other special articles such as this poem. The poem appears with the following preface: 'Dr N.M. O'Donnell writes: The following ballad was composed in 1779, when the rebellion was crushed, and prisoners were being sent in droves across the ocean to "Botany Bay". Its value, either as literature or history, is low, but it is interesting to us in Australian in that these are probably the only Gaelic verses in existence introducing a reference to Australia that were composed in the eighteenth century, and while still Irish was the spoken language of the great majority of the Irish people. The author is unknown.' Dr O'Donnell was self-taught in Irish. He contributed articles to Dublin's *Cladeam Soluis* and was a regular advocate of the Irish language through his contributions to the *Advocate*, including Irish language lessons.

4 See biographical material on Eugene Ryan in Patrick O'Farrell's *The Irish in Australia* (1987) pp. 178/188

5 When I asked at the Conradh na Gaeilge office in Dublin no one had heard of this 'dictionary'.

6 Vincent Woods' translation into English appears on page 257 of *The Turning Wave*.

GLOSSARY

I have used Diarmaid Ó Muirithe's *A Dictionary of Anglo-Irish* as the primary reference in the compilation of this Glossary. The Glossary uses the correct Irish spelling for the head word. Each word is given a chronology from the earliest text of this research in which it was cited to the latest text. The first date of publication of a work is used for the chronology of the words. This provides a useful history of Irish language words in Australian writing and makes it possible to see the development in spelling of particular words over time. Individual words are presented as part of a sentence or phrase. Sentences of dialogue are presented in inverted commas. The absence of inverted commas means the sentence is part of the narrative.

A chara voc. phr. 'my friend'. The usual way of addressing somebody in a letter. **1991** Vincent Buckley, *Last Poems* 189: 'A chara, I'm sorry'.

A/mo chroí voc. phr. 'my heart'. As **achree, chree, mo chree**. **1857** Anonymous, 'Paddy's Letter' in *Old Bush Songs* 64: 'If not, it's small comfort that you have, achree!'; **1882** Mary Fortune, *The Fortunes of Mary Fortune* 85: 'if it isn't yourself a' the darlin' asthore machree of a b'y!'; **1908** James Harbinson, 'Opum Furiosa Cupido' in *Love Lyrics* 51: cuisle mo chroidhe; **1926** Marion Miller Knowles, *Pierce O'Grady's Daughter* 71: 'Aunt Machree!'; **1928** Marion Miller Knowles, *Pretty Nan Hartigan* 49: 'mother machree'; **1928** Marion Miller Knowles, *Pretty Nan Hartigan* 49: 'You're always right, mother machree'; **1928** Brent of Bin Bin, *Up The Country* 71: 'Cushla ma chree, Oim woild for a little advinture'/ 165: 'Don't cry, Emily, my chree'; **1945** William Carty, 'Carrowbehy' in *The Waves of Cool-a-vin* 7: And the warmest welcomes from gra' mo chree. Glossed as: Gradh mo chroidhe. Grah mo chree – Love of my heart.

A/mo chuisle voc phr. 'oh/my pulse'. In forms **acushla, macushla, cushla, macush**. **1845** James Tucker, *Ralph Rashleigh* 120: 'Why thin acushla,'; **1903** Tom Collins, *Such is Life* 287: 'Macushla, mavourneen,'; **1908** James

Harbinson, 'Acushla' in *Love Lyrics* 50: Acushla (Title); **1916** Mary Grant Bruce, *Jim and Wally* 161: 'If you'd come back to Australia with us, acushla machree'; **1921** 'John O'Brien' 'Tell Me What's A Girl To Do' in *Around The Boree Log* 143: 'Yer', Acushla, but 'tis ketchin'; **1926** Marion Miller Knowles, *Pierce O'Grady's Daughter* 194: 'Cushla Machree'; **1928** Brent of Bin Bin, *Up The Country* 71: 'Cushla ma chree, Oim woild for a little advinture; **1949** Ruth Park, *Poor Man's Orange* 114: 'Easy, acushla!' he said softly; **1963** Criena Rohan, *Down By The Dockside* 165: 'How about that, Macush?'.

A ghrá voc phr. 'my love'. As **agrah**. **1840** Anonymous, 'Mrs O'Keefe's Adventures in Australia' in *Old Bush Songs* 64: 'When the masther found out that my block it was short, agrah!'; **1845** James Tucker, *Ralph Rashleigh* 176: 'What sort of a man is he, agrah?'; **1867** Charles De Boos, *Fifty Years Ago* 272: 'Did ye quiet him Ted agrah?'; **1999** Christopher Koch, *Out of Ireland* 454: 'Robert, a-ghrá,' she will say.

A leanbh voc phr. 'my child'. As **alanna, alannah**. **1845** James Tucker, *Ralph Rashleigh* 120: 'Well thin, alanna'; **1867** Charles De Boos, *Fifty Years Ago* 253: 'It's too good a thing, alannah, to let slip off so aisy as that'; **1882** Mary Fortune, *The Fortunes Of Mary Fortune* 45: 'A follyin' 'em iver since the first month, alanna'; **1921** 'John O'Brien' 'The Parting Rosary' in *Around The Boree Log* 128: They've been cruel times, alannah; **1926** Marion Miller Knowles, *Pierce O'Grady's Daughter* 7: 'Judy, alanna'; **1928**, Brent of Bin Bin, *Up The Country* 25: 'Sure ye've done right, Alannah'; **1948** Eleanor Dark, *Storm of Time* 58: 'Oh can ye see, alannah'; **1949** Ruth Park, *Poor Man's Orange* 71: 'Not on here alanna, because I've scrubbed the floor'; **1950** Will Lawson and Tom Hickey, *Moira of Green Hills* 142: 'So rest easy alannah'; **1963** Criena Rohan, *Down by the Dockside* 21: 'You'll be alright, alannah'.

A mhic voc phr. 'oh son'. In forms **avich, avick. 1867** Charles De Boos, *Fifty Years Ago* 281: 'an' now Roger avich, we'll be afther turning in'; **1919** Marion Miller Knowles, *The Little Doctor* 118: 'Bless you avick'; **1926** Marion Miller Knowles, *Pierce O'Grady's Daughter* 20: 'our own ways must change with them, avick'; **1928** Marion Miller Knowles, *Pretty Nan Hartigan* 7: 'she's too young for the like of you, Danny avic!'.

A/mo mhuirnín n. 'my/oh little darling'. In forms **avourneen, mavourneen**. **1867** Charles De Boos, *Fifty Years Ago* 332: 'Divil a much Christian in that, avourneen'; **1903** Tom Collins, *Such is Life* 287: 'Macushla, mavourneen'; **1908** James Harbinson, 'Opum Furiosa Cupido' in *Love Lyrics* 64: Come into the twilight/Mavourneen!; **1909** Bernard O'Dowd, 'Australia Mavourneen' in *Collected Poems of Bernard O'Dowd* 177: Australia mavourneen, my heather, my rose!; **1912** Mary Grant Bruce, *Glen Eyre* 187: 'Tell him I'm comin' before long at all, mavourneen'; **1925** Josephine Anstead, *The Son of the Bondswoman* 11: 'you don't love me, mavourneen'; **1926** Marion Miller Knowles, *Pierce O'Grady's Daughter* 31: 'Katty Mavourneen'; **1928** Brent of Bin Bin, *Up The Country* 155 : 'Sure the she-rogue has more pluck than two of ye, Larry Mavourneen'; **1943** Miles Franklin, *All That Swagger* 4: 'Johanna, Mavourneen!'; **1956** Mavis Thorpe Clark, *The Brown Land was Green* 132: 'Now it's a hand-up I'll need, mavourneen.'; **1995** Thomas Keneally, *Homebush Boy* 32: And if you didn't he would come down and ironically call you mavourneen.

A rún voc phr. 'oh secret'. As **aroon**. **1919** Marion Miller Knowles, *The Little Doctor* 197: 'Oh! Sheila aroon'.

A stór voc. phr. 'oh treasure'. As **astore, asthore, ashthore**. **1882** Mary Fortune, *The Fortunes of Mary Fortune* 65: 'Oych! come an at wance, ashthore'; **1908** James Harbinson, 'Opum Furiosa Cupido' in *Love Lyrics* 50: Now this little Jewel! Asthore! Asthore!; **1913** J.R. Houlding, *Christopher Cockle's Australian Experiences* 264: 'An' long life to yer, Paddy, asthore'; **1926** Marion Miller Knowles, *Pierce O'Grady's Daughter* 9: 'God bless you for that same, astore'; **1928** Brent of Bin Bin, *Up The Country* 167: 'he's dearer than me own heart to me, Asthore'; **1943** Miles Franklin, *All That Swagger* 164: 'Ye're the deep wan, Molly ashtore.'.

Adh n. 'luck'. In phr. 'may God grant you luck'. **1961** William J. Laubenstein, *The Emerald Whaler* 74: 'go gcuiridh Dia an t-a'dh ort'.

Aeríocht n. 'open air festival'. **1998** Kerry Murphy, *Kerry Murphy's Memoirs* 325: Irish dancing, a brass band and an annual Aeridheacht over many years.

Aililiú interj. 'an exclamation of surprise or sorrow'. **1945** William Carty, 'Aililiu' in *The Waves of Cool-a-vin*, 15: Aililiu! but it's lonely. Glossed as: El-il-yew, Alas!

Aisling n. 1. 'a vision', vision poem'. **1943** Miles Franklin, *All That Swagger* 304: that aisling sense of his forefathers which personifies Ireland as the Dark Rosaleen; **1999** Christopher Koch, *Out of Ireland* 164: Barry told me this was an aisling, or vision-song.

Ainneseoir n. 'miserable person'. As **angashore**. **1954** 'John O'Brien', 'Sittin' Be The Wall' in *The Parish of St Mel's* 101: just a crabbed little angashore who was once hard as steel. Glossed as: A miserable little creature.

Aisteach n. in phr. 'Isn't that peculiar?'. **1999** Christopher Koch, *Out of Ireland* 568: 'nach aisteach é sin'.

Amadán n. 'fool'. As **omadhaun, omethaun, omathaun**. **1867** Charles De Boos, *Fifty Years Ago* 238: 'it was small chance the omadhaun ever had of disobeying again'; **1882** Mary Fortune, *The Fortunes of Mary Fortune* 46: 'Git out, ye lot o' crazy omethauns an' square it in the road!'; **1906** A B Paterson *An Outback Marriage* 33: an Omadhaun is a man who began life with some sense; **1908** E.S. Sorenson, *The Squatter's Ward* 277: 'Musha, can't yes hear me, yer omadhaun?'; **1916** Mary Grant Bruce, *Jim and Wally* 113: 'Bad enough for me to be such an omadhaun'; **1923** J.H.M. Abbott, *Sydney Cove* 156: 'a lousy omadhaun like y'silf'; **1926** Marion Miller Knowles, *Pierce O'Grady's Daughter* 20: 'Sorra one of them omathauns'; **1928** Marion Miller Knowles, *Pretty Nan Hartigan* 14: 'you omadhaun you! 175: 'ye pair of blundering omathauns!'; **1950** Will Lawson and Tom Hickey, *Moira of Green Hills* 97: 'Miss, I've waited for this day to tell these unbelievin' omadhauns the truth about Oireland.'

An ea inter. phr. 'is it?'. As **inyagh**. **1882** Mary Fortune, *The Fortunes of Mary Fortune* 71: 'Bether man inyagh! Show him to me!'.

Ara interj. 'ah!'. As **arr, arrah, arra, erra, gerrah, yerra, yerrah**. **1840** Anonymous, 'Paddy Malone in Australia' in *Old Bush Songs* 58: 'Arrah, Paddy Malone!; **1840** 'Frank the Poet', 'A Dialogue Between Two Hibernians at Botany Bay' in *Old Bush Songs* 29: 'Yerra, well I know'; **1840** Anonymous, 'Mrs O'Keefe's Adventures in Australia' in *Old Bush Songs* 63: 'Arrah, mother', sis I'; **1845** James Tucker, *Ralph Rashleigh* 100: 'Employ yeos? Gerrah, thin, why not?'; **1847** Edward Landor, *The Bushman* 147: 'Arrah, and it's a fine baste that same'; **1849** Alexander Harris, *The Emigrant Family* 108: 'Arrah, bad luck to ye's'; **1855** William Howitt, *Land, Labour and Gold* 284: 'Arrah! but the tailor was a clever fellow'; 1859 William Kelly, *Life in Victoria* 279: 'Arrah, be japers!'; **1865** Ellen Davitt, *Force and Fraud* 21: 'Arrah! and d'ye think I'd be bothering myself with another girl'; **1867** Charles De Boos, *Fifty Years Ago* 294: 'Arrah, wait a while, Lanty!'; **1882** Mary Fortune, *The Fortunes of Mary Fortune* 63: 'Arrah, why wouldn't I git here as well as anyone?'; **1903** Tom Collins, *Such is Life* 368: 'Arrah, fwy wud the chap call on the Daity?'; **1908** E.S. Sorenson, *The Squatter's Ward* 342: 'Arra, musha, he's cheated me too'; **1912** Mary Grant Bruce, *Glen Eyre* 150: 'yerrah, here's tat woman!', 171: 'Arrah, I don't mind'; **1913** J.R. Houlding, *Christopher Cockle's Australian Experiences* 48: 'Arra! lift up your head a bit'; **1916** Mary Grant Bruce, *Jim and Wally* 59: 'Yerra, if I could fight'; **1919** J.H.M. Abbott, *The Governor's*

Man 90: 'Arrah now, don't be tellin' me'; **1926** Marion Miller Knowles, *Pierce O'Grady's Daughter* 23: 'Arrah, can't ye keep your big feet in the air'; **1928** Marion Miller Knowles, *Pretty Nan Hartigan* 14: 'Arrah, is it putting the sore heart into a sadly sore body you want to be doing', 37: 'Yerra, don't tell me'; **1930** Henry Handel Richardson, *The Fortunes of Richard Mahony* 20: 'Arrah, an' is it yerrself, Purdy, me bhoy?'; **1943** Miles Franklin, *All That Swagger* 10: Danny 'arrahed' at ghosts; **1947** Frank Clune, *Ben Hall* 23: 'Arrah, Johnny, me bhoy': **1948** Eleanor Dark, *Storm of Time* 505: 'Arrah, it's not so aisy'; **1954** 'John O'Brien','Sittin' Be the Wall' in *The Parish of St Mel's* 103: Yerra thin, unless I'm dreamin. 'tis yourself that's dancin' there,/ 110: Erra, "Afterwards", how are you!; **1960** Donald McLean, *The Roaring Days* 140: 'Arr! I'll call me wife Bridget'; **1996** Ann Clancy, *The Wild Colonial Girl* 74: 'Arrah, there are more starts here than in the whole of Ireland'; **2001** Peter Carey, *True History of the Kelly Gang* 109: Arrah nonesense my mother said.

Bairín breac n. 'speckled loaf'. As **barm brack**. **1979** Vincent Buckley, *The Pattern* 23: Barm brack, soda bread.

Bán n. 'lea; grassland'. As **bawn**. **1979** Vincent Buckley, *The Pattern* 25: each cabin inside its bawn.

Banbh n. 'piglet'. In form **bonniv**. **1916** Mary Grant Bruce, *Jim and Wally* 168: 'and the bonnivs under the wheels of him'.

Bastún n. 'lout, poltroon, blockhead'. In form **bosthoon**. **1906** A B Paterson, *An Outback Marriage* 33: A Bosthoon being a man who never had any great amount of sense. **1908** E.S. Sorenson, *The Squatter's Ward* 264: 'Musha, there's not a bosthoon can bate him at tellin' the truth by contraries'.

Bean feasa n. 'wise woman, fortune-teller'. **1999** Jill Blee, *Brigid* 180: 'the bean feasa was gone'.

Bean sí n. Literally, 'woman of the fairies'. A being who was said to predict death in some Irish families. In form **banshee**. **1874** Marcus Clarke, *For the Term of His Natural Life* 126: 'You never hear the story of the 'Banshee'?; **1886** Fergus Hume, *Mystery of the Hansom Cab* 65: 'I'd much rather listen to our ancient Banshee'; **1900** Robert Bruce, *Benbonuna* 25: a sound long-drawn and dismal enough for the cry of a banshee; **1924** Jack Bradshaw, *Highway Robbery Under Arms* 119: 'What in the name of hell, or the banshees of ould Ireland'; **1926** Marion Miller Knowles, *Pierce O'Grady's Daughter* 71: 'such weird banshee wails'; **1927** Alice Guerin Crist 'The Banshee' in *When Rody Came to Ironbark* 60: The Banshee (Title); **1943**

Miles Franklin, *All That Swagger* 132: 'I had to take banshees for me familiars and become the aquil of black haythens for want of better company'; **1945** William Carty, 'The Fall of the Year' in *The Waves of Cool-a-vin* 20: With a cry like a lone ban-shee; **1948** Eleanor Dark, *Storm of Time* 557: 'an' she shriekin' like a Banshee!'; **1959** Mary Durack, *Kings in Grass Castles* 50: the Australian curlew was always the banshee wail of her native bogs; **1965** Leslie Haylen, *Big Red* 12: and whistled along the ground like a banshee; **1998** Thomas Keneally, *The Great Shame* 333: They ran in with what Meagher called a banshee shriek; **1999** Michael Meehan, *The Salt of Broken Tears* 284: 'and she beginning to talk but like the banshee my husband always said she was'; **1999** Christopher Koch, *Out of Ireland* 267: 'She believes in the banshee'; **1999** Jill Blee, *Brigid* 159: 'they came a-wailing up to the village like a pack of bean sí'; **2000** Peter Carey, *True History of the Kelly Gang* 98: The Banshee made no answer.

Bean tí n. 'housewife'. As **vanithee**. **1998** Thomas Keneally, *The Great Shame* 244: seemed to be the characteristic vanithee, or woman of the house.

(Mo) Bhrón int. 'my sorrow'. Also as **mavrone**. **1945** William Carty, 'Spring' in *The Waves of Cool-a-vin* 34: The birds make love in the boughs, mavrone! **1999** Christopher Koch, *Out of Ireland* 259: 'Ah, mo bhrón!' she said.

Bia cladaigh n. 'shell-fish'. **1999** Jill Blee, *Brigid* 33: 'And a bit of herring and the bia cladough'.

Bia na mbocht n. 'food of the poor'. **1999** Jill Blee, *Brigid* 33: Bia na mbacht! Food from the sea. Poor man's food'.

Bó interj. 'alas!'. As **vo**. **1882** Mary Fortune, *The Fortunes of Mary Fortune* 72: 'Oh vo,vo'.

Bodhrán n. 'kind of tambourine'. **1991** Vincent Buckley, 'How The Irish Speak Pentameters' in *Last Poems* 37: of the man who partnered them on bodhrán.

Bóithrín n. 'small road'. In form **boreen**. **1855** William Howitt, *Land, Labour and Gold* 274: the Giant King Brian Boreen; **1908** James Harbinson, 'Opum Furiosa Cupido' in *Love Lyrics* 50: We met in a shady boihreen, boihreen; **1916** Mary Grant Bruce, *Jim and Wally* 115: but the boreen was all in shade; **1927** Alice Guerin Crist, 'West of Fanny O'Deas's' in *When Rody Came to Ironbark* 22: The fairies lurk in the boreens there; **1954** 'John O'Brien', 'The Meeting' in *The Parish of St Mel's* 33: There came the smell of new-mown hay along the old boreen; **1994** Tim Winton, *The Riders* 14: from windows and barns and muddy boreens; **1999** Jill Blee, *Brigid* 44: 'Go down the bóithrín'.

Bréidín n. 'home-spun woollen cloth'. As **breadeen**. **1996** David Malouf, *The Conversations at Curlew Creek* 167: They had slept on fresh rushes and bundles of woollen breadeen.

Breacast n. 'breakfast'. As **bregguest**. **1845** James Tucker, *Ralph Rashleigh* 118: 'get together summat for bregguest'.

Bróg n. 'shoe, boot'. In form **brogue**. Diminutive **bróigín**, as **brogueen, brogan**. **1840** Anonymous, 'Mrs O'Keefe's Adventures in Australia' in *Old Bush Songs* 63: And no brogues to his trotters; **1845** James Tucker, *Ralph Rashleigh* 103: 'if he hasn't brought me Nancy's little brogueens (small shoes) instead of my own'; **1859** William Kelly, *Life in Victoria* 138: Even Pat himself...was come to for a few pairs of stout brogues; **1890** 'Banjo' Paterson, 'The Tug-of-War' in *The World of 'Banjo' Paterson* 128: planted their brogues against the battens; **1913** J.R. Houlding, *Christopher Cockle's Australian Experiences* 123: 'wid a broad new pair of brogans'; **1986** Térése Radic, 'Extracts from a Half Breed's Diary' in *Sweet Mothers, Sweet Maids* 116: No one dances in competition brogues on the dusty stage.

Brú n. 'dwelling'. As **brugh**. **1945** William Carty, *The Waves of Cool-a-vin* 12: I followed her for love/To her brugh in the moon-white hour. Glossed as Brugh-Broo, Fairy mansion.

Brúitín n. 'mashed potatoes mixed with onion and butter'. As **bruitin**. **2000** Peter Carey, *True History of the Kelly Gang* 42: what my father called BRUITIN and the Quinns called CHAMP.

Buachaill n. 'boy', young man'. In forms **bouhal, bouchal**. **1867** Charles De Boos, *Fifty Years Ago* 251: 'An' ye won't stand no more, won't ye ma bouchal'; **1921** 'John O'Brien' 'The Parting Rosary' in *Around The Boree Log* 130: O'h I'm thankin' God, my bouhal. Glossed as: Boy; also spelt bouchal; **1998** Kerry Murphy, *Kerry Murphy's Memoirs* 230: Maith an Bhuchaill, A Mhuiris!

Cach bó coined n. from cach 'excrement' and bó 'cow'. **1945** William Carty, 'To the Lovers of the Unlovely' in *The Waves of Cool-a-vin* 25: Leave the cac-bo to the beetle. Glossed as Cock-bo, cow-dung.

Cáibín n. 'an old hat'. In form **caubeen**. **1859** William Kelly, *Life in Victoria* Vol 2 168: like a man in a pillory crowned with the dilapidated caubeen. Glossed as: Caubeen in Ireland is understood to mean a smashed hat; **1926** Marion Miller Knowles, *Pierce O'Grady's Daughter* 146: lifting his old caubeen reverently.

Cailín n. 'girl'. As **colleen**. **1829** David Burn, *The Bushrangers* 19: a colleen; **1867** Charles De Boos, *Fifty Years Ago* 262: 'an shure its the colleen dhas she is'/ 262: 'or maybe ye'll be hurting the colleen dhras?'; **1908** James Harbinson, 'Opum Furiosa Cupido' in *Love Lyrics* 50: meself, and me purty Colleen; **1916** Mary Grant Bruce, *Jim and Wally* 167: a fresh and smiling colleen; **1919** J.H.M. Abbott, *The Governor's Man* 131: 'He's welcome to his colleen's letters'; **1924** Jack Bradshaw, *Highway Robbery Under Arms* 20: more beautiful than the Colleen Bawn herself; **1926** Marion Miller Knowles, *Pierce O'Grady's Daughter* 184: 'a little beyond his live for his own colleen'; **1943** Miles Franklin, *All That Swagger* 135: 'After all, 'tis a vaynial sin for the gossoons and colleens to be fond of wan another.'; **1947** Frank Clune, *Ben Hall* 23: 'Who are these pretty colleens ye've brought with ye?'; **1954** 'John O'Brien', 'The Durkins' in *The Parish of St Mel's* 101: 'And the colleen wife he brought across the sea; **1956** Mavis Thorpe Clark, *The Brown Land was Green* 60: they had acquired two red-headed colleens; **1960** Donald McLean, *The Roaring Days* 5: 'She was a bonny, brown-eyed colleen'; **1961** W.E. Fitzhenry in Forward to Steele Rudd's *On Our Selection*: Steele Rudd's mother was Mary Green, a colleen from outside Roscommon; **1988** Eric Willmot, *Pemulwuy The Rainbow Warrior* 96: 'Listen my colleen, there is hope'.

Cailleach n. 'old woman, hag'. **1999** Jill Blee, *Brigid* 159: 'This time the cailleach laid her curse on John Binden Scott and everyone associated with him.'.

Cál ceannann n. 'a mixture of boiled potatoes, chopped leeks and kale'. As **colcannon**. **1916** Mary Grant Bruce, *Jim and Wally* 100: Mrs Moroney gave her lessons in the manufacture of potato-cakes, colcannon; **1999** Christopher Koch, *Out of Ireland* 531: 'We'll eat a dish of cál ceannann together.

Call n. 1. 'right', claim'. **1889** Rolf Boldrewood, *Robbery Under Arms* 304: 'I'd no call to have done the things I have; **1926** Marion Miller Knowles, *Pierce O'Grady's Daughter* 54: 'But Donagh had no call to say the like of those things to you'; **1928** Brent of Bin Bin, *Up The Country* 75: 'You have no call to be so familiar with ex-convicts'; **1949** Ruth Park, *Poor Man's Orange* 82: 'Your mother didn't have any call to go slinging off at me Moe, anyway.'

Canránaí n. 'grumbler'. In form **keownrawning**. Hence canráning, 'grumbling'. **1921** 'John O'Brien' 'The Trimmin's On The Rosary' in *Around The Boree Log* 18: Then "himself" would start keownrawning. Glossed as: 'grumbling' 'grousing'.

Caoineadh nav. 'lamentation for the dead', 'keening'. In form **keening**. **1865** Henry Kingsley, *The Hillyars and the Burtons* 34: 'Was it for this I keened over the cold hearthstone at Garoopna'; **1889** Rolf Boldrewood, *Robbery Under Arms* 113: 'keening' I think they call it; **1892** Francis Adams, *Australian Life* 102: 'They kept on keening to the last'; **1927** Alice Guerin Crist, 'The Banshee' in *When Rody Came to Ironbark* 60: As the shrill keening rang o'erhead; **1928** Marion Miller Knowles, *Pretty Nan Hartigan* 207: 'after all the sorrowful keenin'; **1943** Miles Franklin, *All That Swagger* 304: The keening casuarinas were a voice from another life and drowned him in emotions; **1959** Mary Durack, *Kings in Grass Castles* 92: The keening and praying went on for a day and a night; **1960** Elizabeth O'Connor, *The Irishman* 97: A thin high keening issued from her crumpled lips; **1965** Leslie Haylen, *Big Red* 31: The keening song had a rhythm; **1994** Tim Winton, *The Riders* 74: this was a keening, a cry loaded with desire and remorse; **1998** Thomas Keneally, *The Great Shame* 16: Men shouted curses in Irish, the Larkin women keened; **1999** Michael Meehan, *The Salt of Broken Tears* 51: a silence broken only by the keening of insects; **2000** Peter Carey, *True History of the Kelly Gang* 319: I paid no attention to her keening.

Captaen n. In phr.'are you there captain?'. **1999** Christopher Koch, *Out of Ireland* 531: An bhfuil tú ansin, a Chaptaen?

Carraigín n. 'edible seaweed'. As **Carrigeen**. **1999** Jill Blee, *Brigid* 48: 'Carrigeen moss. It grows in the sea'.

Ceann dubh dílis end. 'dear black head'. As **Cean dhu deelish**. **1926** Marion Miller Knowles, *Pierce O'Grady's Daughter* 34: 'Cean dhu deelish!' he whispered.

Céilí n. 'Irish dancing session'. Also as **ceiledhe**. **1967** Thomas Keneally, *Bring Larks and Heroes* 116: 'It was the way father he danced at Barry's ceili'; **1998** Kerry Murphy, *Kerry Murphy's Memoirs* 272: A Ceiledhe at night sees a full house.

Céirseach n. 'talkative woman'. In form **keerschuch**. **1921** 'John O'Brien' 'Norah O'Neill' in *Around the Boree Log* 96: But he can't for that keerschuch O'Neill.

Ceol beag n. 'small music'. **1979** Vincent Buckley, *The Pattern* 46: to make the CEOL-BEAG.

Cill n. 'church, churchyard'. Also as **cille, kille**. **1916** Mary Grant Bruce, *Jim and Wally* 166: 'So he came to be called Columcille – cille meaning church'; **1945** William Carty, 'Lament for Elwood' in *The Waves of Cool-a-vin* 32: Now, the Chief of Clan Elwood/Is laid in the clay of the kille. Glossed as: Cill (kille) – A churchyard.

Cipín n. 'small stick'. As **kip, kippy, kippen. 1928** Louis Stone, *Jonah* 159: He marked pak-a-pu tickets, took the kip at two-up; **1946** Katherine Susannah Prichard, *The Roaring Nineties* 165: Two were placed tail-up on the kip/ 166: the kippy had put a 'gig' on it; **1959** Mary Durack, *Kings in Grass Castles* 83: 'Now what sort of a kippenhead will be wanting to perch on the roof-top wheniver the creek's in flood?'; **1965** Louis Stone, *Jonah* 159: took the kip at two-up.

Cis n. 'basket'. As **kish. 1916** Mary Grant Bruce, *Jim and Wally* 179: 'She has a kish full of fish'.

Ciseán n. 'wicker basket'. As **rishawn** (sic). **1996** David Malouf, *The Conversations at Curlew Creek* 157: She set her orange in the rishawn beside the two hares.

Clábar n. 'mud'. In forms **clauber, clabber, claubery. 1859** William Kelly, *Life in Victoria* 220: my head, face, beard, and hands were coated with clauber. Glossed as: Clauber is a sort of consistent paste made of mud and moisture, unknown to Johnson; **1930** Henry Handel Richardson, *The Fortunes of Richard Mahony* 11: Their faces were daubed with clauber; **1965** Leslie Haylen *Big Red* 30: 'I don't want to shovel up great clabbers of horse dung in the mornin'; **1945** William Carty, 'The Grey Woods of Doon Gar' in *The Waves of Cool-a-vin* 14: Brown fields and claubery boreens. Glossed as: Claubery-boreens, boggy lanes.

Clachan n. 'cluster of houses'. **1999** Jill Blee, *Brigid* 45: 'A clachan. Farms and houses, that's all it was'.

Cóisir n. 'gossiping'. In forms **cothering, coshering. 1867** Charles De Boos, *Fifty Years Ago* 252: 'cothering and colloguering together'/ 370: 'coshering and collogueing together'.

Corcaigh n. Cork city. **1978** Richard Butler, *Against the Wind* 23: one couple road all the way from Corcaigh itself – Cork; as the English called it.

Craic n. 'fun'. As **crack. 1998** Kerry Murphy, *Kerry Murphy's Memoirs* 332: funny stories were told, as we say the craic was on all the time and still learning Gaelic.

Crotar n 'lichen'. In form **crother. 1998** Thomas Keneally, *The Great Shame* 129: They gathered seaweeds, named crother and dulaman.

Crústaigh v. 'pelting'. As **croosted**. **1998** Kerry Murphy, *Kerry Murphy's Memoirs* 25: and it was often we who croosted (threw) a few sods or keerans at him.

Cúileann n. 'fair maiden'. As **coolun**. **1945** William Carty, 'The Linnaun Shee' in *The Waves of Cool-a-vin* 11: And many is the coolun that I courted till the morn. Glossed as: Coolun – Beautiful girl.

Dia n. 'God'. In phrases 'may God prosper you', 'thank God' and 'God save Ireland'. **1961** William J. Laubenstein, *The Emerald Whaler* 74: 'go soirbhi Dia dhuit'; **1998** Kerry Murphy, *Kerry Murphy's Memoirs* 94: And 'Buidhcheas le Dia' both games were a credit to the players/ 232: A Dhia Saor Eire.

Diabhal n. 'the devil'. As **diaoul, dhoul**. In phrase th'anam 'on diabhal 'your soul to the devil'. **1849** Alexander Harris, *The Emigrant Family* 96: 'Anamondyoul!'; Glossed as: Obscure; presumably a phonetic spelling of a corrupt pronunciation; **1867** Charles De Boos, *Fifty Years Ago* 238: 'Anna man diaoul!', cried Lanty/ 272: 'Dhoul!' cried Lanty/ 294: 'Hannin in dhoul!' growled Lanty; **1900** Rolf Boldrewood, *Babes in the Bush* 34: 'But I'll have the heart's blood of ye, if ye were the Diaoul out of h-l.'; **2002** Jill Blee, *The Liberator's Birthday* 94: 'Chun an diabhal leat!'

Droimín n. 'low ridge'. As **drumlin**. **1991** Vincent Buckley 'The Lake' in *Last Poems* 71: the drumlin lifted.

Dúidín n. 'short smoking pipe'. Also in forms **dhudeen, dudeen, dudun**. **1845** James Tucker, *Ralph Rashleigh* 103: who only opened his oracular jaws to emit the smoke of his dhudeen; **1847** Alexander Harris, *Settlers and Convicts* 5: and the dudeen … was in everybody's mouth; **1851** John Henderson, *Excursions and Adventures in New South Wales* vol 2 112: and sometimes an old clay cutty, or dudun; **1859** William Kelly, *Life in Victoria* 140: a short pipe of the true "dudheen breed"; **1913** J.R. Houlding, *Christopher Cockle's Australian Experiences* 256: 'Old Paddy was shmokin' his dudeen on the deck of the sthamer'; **1998** Thomas Keneally, *The Great Shame* 42: convict women … smoking Brazil twist in dudeens, clay pipes sometimes scarcely half and inch long.

Duilisc n. 'lichen'. As **dilisk**. **1999** Jill Blee, *Brigid* 57: 'Not the dilisk, those long streamers you're looking at'.

Dúlamán n. 'channelled wrack'. In form **dulaman**. **1998** Thomas Keneally, *The Great Shame* 129: They gathered seaweeds, named crother and dulaman.

Éire go brách phr. 'Ireland forever'. In form **Erin-go-bragh, Erin go brách**. **1926**

Marion Miller Knowles, *Pierce O'Grady's Daughter* 20: 'Erin-go-bragh for it then'; **1961** William J. Laubenstein, *The Emerald Whaler* 163: 'This chance can never come again. Erin go bragh.'; **1963** Criena Rohan, *Down By The Dockside* 160: a monstrous shamrock, inscribed Erin Go Bragh; **1998** Thomas Keneally, *The Great Shame* 95: the banners stitched in red on green: Erin go bragh; **1998** Kerry Murphy, *Kerry Murphy's Memoirs* 232: Erin Mavourneen, Erin Go Brath; **1999** Christopher Koch, *Out of Ireland* 205: 'Three cheers for the leader of Young Ireland! Erin-go-bragh!'; 531: Éire go brách.

Fág an bealach phr. 'clear the way'. In form **faugh-a-ballagh**. **1854** G.R. Nichols, *Sydney Revels* 31: 'poor Faugh-a-ballagh savage!'; **1859** William Kelly, *Life in Victoria* 264: Cast any imputation on butter, and faugh-a-ballagh was the shout of the "Double-rose" Cork manufacture; **1998** Thomas Keneally, *The Great Shame* 94: Duffy's poem 'Faugh-a-Ballagh' (Irish for 'Clear the Way') also set the Nation's tone.

Fáilte n. 'welcome'. As **faltagh, failte**. Also in phrase **céad míle fáilte** as **Ceud Mile Failte**, 'a hundred thousand welcomes'. **1845** James Tucker, *Ralph Rashleigh* 120:'Cead mille faltagh! Welcome, kind welcome!; **1994** Tim Winton, *The Riders* 88: Every town said Failte, Welcome to Moneygall, Toomyvara, Nenagh; **1998** Kerry Murphy, *Kerry Murphy's Memoirs* 87: Another great Irish home that always gave us a Ceud Mile Failte was that of Mr and Mrs Woulfe of Lewisham.

Faraor interj. 'alas!'. As **foirior**. **1945** William Carty, 'The Linnaun Shee' in *The Waves of Cool-a-Vin* 12: But yon dreadful night, foirior! haunts, and shall haunt me still. Glossed as: Foirior – Fo-reer, alas!

Fear n. 'man'. In phr. 'I'm your man!'. **1999** Christopher Koch, *Out of Ireland* 531: mise an fear agat!

(b') **Féidir** sin In phr. 'perhaps so'. In form **bothershion**. **1867** Charles De Boos, *Fifty Years Ago* 271: 'Och, bothershion!'.

Feis n. 'festival'. Also as **Feiseanna** (pl). **1943** Miles Franklin, *All That Swagger* 50: Enlivened by the feis, Johanna turned with fresh heart to her tasks; **1998** Kerry Murphy, *Kerry Murphy's Memoirs* 41: Today there are music festivals or Feisanna held all over Ireland.

Fia n. 'kill'. **1996** David Malouf, *The Conversations at Curlew Creek* 153: 'look a' the fiadh.'.

Fiabhras buí n. 'Yellow fever'. 1998 Thomas Keneally, *The Great Shame* 112: It was sometimes named Yellow Fever, fiabhras buidhe.

Fiabhras dubh n. 'Typhus'. **1998** Thomas Keneally, *The Great Shame* 111: Esther saw the emergence of what people called Black Fever, fiabhras dubh

Fleá Ceoil n. 'musical festival'. **1998** Kerry Murphy, *Kerry Murphy's Memoirs* 41: There are musical competitions called Fleadh Ceol.

Fústar v. 'fuss, fidgeting'. As **footering**. **1954** 'John O'Brien', 'Sittin' Be the Wall' in *The Parish of St Mel's* 104: That's him footering in the shadows.

Gaeilge n. Ling: 'Irish'. In phrase 'don't you speak Irish?/You don't have any Irish then?'. **1999** Christopher Koch, *Out of Ireland* 568: 'Nach labhrann tú Gaeilge?'/'Níl Gaeilge ar bith agat, mar sin; **1999** Jill Blee, *Brigid* 115: Gaeilge (Chapter heading).

Gaeltachtaí n. 'Irish-speaking areas'. **1979** Vincent Buckley, *The Pattern* 10: Many Gaeltachts.

Gaimbín n. 'usurer'. As **gombeen**. **1859** William Kelly, *Life in Victoria* 320: The one he purchased at a usurious rate from the gombeen man. Glossed as: Gombeen man is an Irish character – a village usurer, who sells out food and seed at exorbitant rates, taking advantage of the necessities of the poor; **1991** Vincent Buckley, 'Looking Down Thomas Street' in *Last Poems* 84: son of Gombeen.

Gamach n. 'simpleton, clown'. In form **gommach**. **1900** Rolf Boldrewood, *Babes in the Bush* 343: 'Was there ever such a gommach!'.

Gardaí n. 'guards'. **1996** Jill Blee, *Brigid* 191: There are only two gardaí in Ballyvaghan.

Garsún n. 'boy'. As **gossoon.** **1845** James Tucker, *Ralph Rashleigh* 176: 'And oughtn't I to know him whin we used to be gossoons together playing at hurley in ould Ireland'; **1847** Edward Landor, *The Bushman* 143: Mike had sprouted out into a fine gossoon of a boy; **1854** G.R. Nichols, *Sydney Revels* 69: 'and then passes my hand to the other gossoon'; **1865** Ellen Davitt, *Force and Fraud* 38: 'I've known ye ever since ye were a bit of a ragged gossoon', Glossed: gossoon, Anglo-Irish word derived from French garcon, describing a serving boy, lackey, or silly awkward fellow; **1867** Charles De Boos, *Fifty Years Ago* 341: 'it's a dale more I do be knowing of that gossoon'; **1900** Rolf Boldrewood, *Babes in the Bush* 345: 'and him helpless with that gossoon in his arms'; **1908** E.S. Sorenson, *The Squatter's Ward* 343: 'Arrah, it's the gossoon wid the ponies.'; **1913** J.R. Houlding, *Christopher Cockle's Australian Experiences* 30: 'as the Earl of Munster's flunkey said to the gossoon'; **1916** Mary Grant Bruce, *Jim and*

Wally 137: 'I left a bit of a gossoon to mind the shop'; **1919** Marion Miller Knowles, *The Little Doctor* 117: 'ask the doctor if he'd like to see a foot-sore gossoon named Mortimer'; **1921** 'John O'Brien', 'Moryah' in *Around The Boree Log* 139: And the chubby gossoon with dart; **1926** Marion Miller Knowles, *Pierce O'Grady's Daughter* 23: 'Ye gawk of a gossoon'; **1928** Brent of Bin Bin, *Up The Country* 69: 'And phwat bhrings ye two gossoons over'; **1943** Miles Franklin, *All That Swagger* 135: 'After all, 'tis a vaynial sin for the gossoons and colleens to be fond of wan another'; **1962** Frank Bruno, *Fury at Finnegan's Folly* 90: 'an' me but a gossoon knee-high to the pig himself.'; **1946** J.H.M. Abbott, *Red O'Shaughenessy* 127: 'I've had to do wid horses since I was a bit of a gossoon'; **1948** Eleanor Dark, *Storm of Time* 540: 'A lad, Sir, sixteen or thereabouts, an' two little gossoons'.

Gé n. 'goose'. In phr. The Wild Geese (Irish History). As **na Géana Fiáina**. **1978** Richard Butler, *Against The Wind* 29: 'our fathers called them na Gaean Fiadhaine'.

Geasa n. 'spells'. **1998** Thomas Keneally, *The Great Shame* 22: The water of holy wells protected the individual soul from curses or fairy tricks, and from Geasa Dravidacht, the sorcery of the Druids.

Girseach n. 'young girl'. In form **girsha**. **1926** Marion Miller Knowles, *Pierce O'Grady's Daughter* 8: 'The girsha has been shockingly spoiled'; **1928** Marion Miller Knowles, *Pretty Nan Hartigan* 9: bit of a girsha.

Gob n. 'beak, bill, mouth'. **1928** Brent of Bin Bin, *Up The Country* 153: 'Hold your gob!'; **1955** D'Arcy Niland, *The Shiralee* 21: 'Nearly scalded me gob off, that's all'; **1948** Ruth Park, *The Harp in the South* 105: 'You shut yer big gob, Mr Diamond!' cried Mumma stoutly.

Gorta n. 'hunger, famine'. In phr. The Great Famine. **1998** Thomas Keneally, *The Great Shame* 110: The time had begun to which the Irish applied the name an Gorta Mór – the Great Hunger.

Hububú n. 'confused crying or wailing'. As **hubabuboo**. **1829** David Burn, *The Bushrangers* 32: 'you saucy little devil with your hubabuboo'.

Láí n. 'long narrow-bladed spade'. In form **loy**. **1945** William Carty, 'The Fall of the Year' in *The Waves of Cool-a-vin* 20: That knows not loy from plough. Glossed as: Loy – A spade; **1998** Thomas Keneally, *The Great Shame* 20: out with spades called loys.

Leannán sí n. 'fairy lover'. As **liannaun shee**. **1945** William Carty 'The Linnaun Shee' in *The Waves of Cool-a-vin* 11: The Linnaun Shee (Title) Glossed as: Leanan Sidhe (Linnaun Shee) or fairy sweetheart.

Leithéid n. 'likeness'. In phr. 'his like will never be seen again'. **1998** Kerry Murphy, *Kerry Murphy's Memoirs* 318: He is spoken of with respect and sadness, Ni Bheidh A Leitheid Ann Go Deo.

Leipreachán n. 'little fairy man'. In form **leprechaun**. **1919** J.H.M. Abbott, *The Governor's Man* 17: 'an' this little leprechaun here'; 1965 Leslie Haylen, *Big Red* 20: 'livin' here like a leprechaun'.

Leor n. 'sufficiency'. In phr 'that's enough'. **2002** Jill Blee, *The Liberator's Birthday* 236: 'Is leor shin!'

Lios n. 'fairy fort'. As **liss**. **1945** William Carty, 'The Piper of Drimacoo' in *The Waves of Cool-a-vin* 9: An airy place, a fairy place/Is the liss at Carrowrae. Glossed as: Lios – Liss, a faery fort.

Loch n. 'lake'. In form **lough**. **1999** Jill Blee, *Brigid* 209: 'the people had taken to fishing in the lough to ease their hunger'.

Madra n. 'dog'. In phr. 'Do you like the dog? We'll give you the dog'. **2002** Jill Blee, *The Liberator's Birthday* 58: 'An maith leat an madra? Tugaimid an madra duit'.

Maith go leor phr. 'of a drinker, tipsy'. In form **mogolore** **1954** 'John O'Brien', 'Cooney's Daughter' in *The Parish of St Mel's* 111: As he stammered out the speeches, and he mogalore. Glossed as: Half tipsy.

Mar dhea phr. 'as it were, supposedly'. In form **moryah**. **1921** 'John O'Brien', 'Moryah' in *Around The Boree Log* 139: 'Ar', Old Man, but he's yardin'/the cow'. Moryah! Glossed as: 'Moryah is the Celtic equivalent of "I don't think"'; **1954** 'John O'Brien', 'When the "Sut" Drops Down' in The Parish of St Mel's 46: But Bridgie says that's 'all moryah' Glossed as: Fiddlesticks!

Mí-ádh n. 'bad luck'. As **meaw**. **1954** 'John O'Brien', 'When the "Sut" Drops Down' in *The Parish of St Mel's* 104: For there's some "meaw" upon him since the day she married Leary. Glossed as: Ill luck.

Míle n. 'thousand.' In form **meila**. **1882** Mary Fortune, *The Fortunes of Mary Fortune* 72: 'meila murther! meila murther!'

Min n. 'cornmeal'. In phr. 'beggar's cornmeal'. **1998** Thomas Keneally, *The Great Shame* 110: yellow cornmeal which the Irish called 'Peel's brimstone', min déirce, beggar's meal.

Móidín n. 'devout, pious person'. In form **voteen**. **1921** 'John O'Brien', 'Josephine' in *Around The Boree Log* 65: And entertain with parish chat each gossiping voteen. Glossed as: 'A person who exaggerates his or her religious devotion.'

Muire n. interj. 'the personal name confined to the Blessed Virgin Mary'. In forms **wirrah, whirra, wurra wisha, muise, musha, murra, ouisha, isha**. **1829** David Burn, *The Bushrangers* 33: 'Och, musha, it's himself that's the dacent boy, anyhow'; **1840** 'Frank the Poet', 'A Dialogue Between Two Hibernians at Botany Bay' in *Old Bush Songs* 28: 'Musha, welcome to Botany'; **1845** James Tucker, *Ralph Rashleigh* 101: 'Musha now', 117: 'Wirrah! Wirrah!; **1849** Alexander Harris, *The Emigrant Family* 96: 'Musha! bad luck to him every day he rises.'; **1867** Charles De Boos, *Fifty Years Ago* 328: 'Musha thin, there's shmall fun there'd be in that'/ 334: 'Oh wurra what will I do?'; **1882** Mary Fortune, *The Fortunes of Mary Fortune* 113: 'Arra, wisha, Misther Grieve'; **1908** E.S. Sorenson, *The Squatter's Ward* 264: 'Musha, can't yes hear me'; **1913** J.R. Houlding *Christopher Cockle's Australian Experiences* 316: 'Och musha!'; **1916** Mary Grant Bruce, *Jim and Wally* 168: 'Oh, wirra, it's desthroyed she'll be'; **1919** Marion Miller Knowles, *The Little Doctor* 106: 'Isha, hear him!'; **1921** 'John O'Brien', 'Moryah' in *Around The Boree Log* 140: 'Ouisha, Poor old woman, 'tis dreamin' you are'; **1921** 'John O'Brien' 'Tell Me What's A Girl To Do' in *Around The Boree Log* 144: 'Wisha, Mary, don't be talkin'; **1925** Josephine Ansted, *The Son of the Bondswoman* 19: 'whirra, you must be tired'; 1926 Marion Miller Knowles, *Pierce O'Grady's Daughter* 22: 'Isha, won't he be the grand man entirely?'; **1928** Marion Miller Knowles, *Pretty Nan Hartigan* 9: 'But, isha, what is Nan but a childeen in her heart'; **1938** Xavier Herbert, *Capricornia* 156: 'Oh wirrah man wirrah!'; **1943** Miles Franklin, *All That Swagger* 27: 'Murra me, that ever I was born and came roaming to the wilds!'; **1946** H M Abbott, *Red O'Shaughenessy* 179: 'Oh, wirra, wirra - an' him dead in the twinkle of an eye'; **1946** Katherine Susannah Prichard, *The Roaring Nineties* 304: 'Wisher, wisher, God bless us,'; **1954** 'John O'Brien', 'Sittin' Be The Wall' *The Parish of St Mel's* 104: 'Wisha thin, 'tis well I mind her'; **1999** Christopher Koch, *Out of Ireland* 'Muise nach aisteach é sin'.

(A) **Mhuire is trua** phr. 'O Mary and pity'. In form **Wirristrue**. **1945** William Carty, 'At Evantide' in *The Waves of Cool-a-vin* 140: This night nor any night, – Ah! Wirristrue.

Ochón interj. 'Alas!'. Also in forms **ochone, ohone, och hon**. **1840** Anonymous, 'Paddy Malone in Australia' in *Old Bush Songs* 'Sure I don't know it now I'm so bothered, Ohone!; **1845** James Tucker, *Ralph Rashleigh* 124 'Ochone! Ochone! mother darlint'; **1860** Mary Theresa Vidal, *Bengala* 242: 'Och hon, Och hon!'; **1908** James Harbinson, 'Opum Furiosa Cupido' in *Love Lyrics* 50: Och! She is a darlint, ahone, Ahone!; **1913** J.R. Houlding,

Christopher Cockle's Australian Experiences 100: 'Ochone! it's enough to drive any raysinable man clane cranky'; **1928** Brent of Bin Bin, *Up The Country* 69: 'Och hone, I knew it!'; **1962** Frank Bruno, *Fury at Finnegan's Folly* 159: 'Ochone, the sorrow of ut!'.

Paltóg n. 'blow, thump'. In forms **polthogue, poltough**. **1840** Anonymous, 'Mrs O'Keefe's Adventures in Australia' in *Old Bush Songs* 64: I got a polthogue from a blackfella's waddy then; **1854** G.R. Nichols, *Sydney Revels* 65: 'And Miss Darby runs at me vid de broom, and hits me a polthoge on de shouldur'; **1867** Charles De Boos, *Fifty Years Ago* 271: 'bad luck to his washy head that couldn't stand a poltough from a gun stock'.

Pililiú interj. 'an exclamation of surprise or sorrow'. As **philleloo**. **1913** J.R. Houlding, *Christopher Cockle's Australian Experiences* 52: 'If any mortail man in the worrld iver heard a bigger phillelloo nor this'.

Poc amach v. 'kick out'. Phr in the game of hurling. As **pucked**. **1998** Kerry Murphy, *Kerry Murphy's Memoirs* 93: watching a ball being pucked out by a man, bred, born and reared near Thurles or Mooncoin.

Póiríní n. 'small potatoes'. As **poreens**. **1945** William Carty, 'The Grey Woods of Doon Gar' in *The Waves of Cool-a-vin* 14: Full of yellow grain and poreens. Glossed as: Poreens – Small potatoes.

Poitín n. 'illicit whiskey'. Also in forms **poteen, potheen, pocheen**. **1900** Rolf Boldrewood, *Babes in the Bush* 8: 'If ye won't take any more potheen, let us sleep on it'; **1908** E.S. Sorenson, *The Squatter's Ward* 343: 'the sorra a wan can thrate ye to a betther noggin o' poteen.'; **1947** Frank Clune, *Ben Hall* 22: Paddy's poteen was an irresistible lure; **1950** Will Lawson and Tom Hickey, *Moira of Green Hills* 54: 'No cattle and no sheep–just crops, with some potheen thrown in'; **1959** Mary Durack, *Kings In Grass Castles* 29: 'Himself' found compensation for the bitter restriction of his tenancy in the production of ...'potheen'; **1962** Frank Bruno, *Fury at Finnegan's Folly* 50: Uncle Barney (B.A. Trinity) the schoolteacher, with the pocheen of an evening irrigating the soul of him; **1994** Tim Winton, *The Riders* 37: 'Have you been drinking that poteen again?'; **1996** David Malouf, *The Conversations at Curlew Creek* 165: tossing down an inch or two of harsh-tasting poteen; **1999** Jill Blee, *Brigid* 34: 'Them with their poitín buried in the peat'; **2000** Peter Carey, *True History of the Kelly Gang* 46: It's Grandma Quinn's poteen I said; **2002** Jill Blee, *The Liberator's Birthday* 40: He used to see a bit of poitín.

Priompallán n. 'dung beetle'. As **primperlan**. **1945** William Carty, 'The Fall of the Year' in *The Waves of Cool-a-vin* 20: And the quiet dusk of even/Drops like the primperlaun. Glossed as: Primperlan – A flying beetle.

Púca n. 'ghost'. As **puca**. **1945** William Carty, 'The Tinkers' in *The Waves of Cool-a-Vin* 8: For thavish or Puca, they don't seem to care. Glossed as: Puca-Pookie (Shakespeare's Puck); **2000** Peter Carey, *True History of the Kelly Gang* 30: like a pooka steals your very soul.

Ráiméis n. 'nonsense'. In form **ramaysh**. **1954** 'John O'Brien', 'When the "Sut" Drops Down' in *The Parish of St Mel's* 46: mere "ramaysh". Glossed as: 'Nonesense!'

Ropaire n. al. **rapaire**. 'cut-purse, robber or thief; a highwayman'. In form rapparee. **1900** Rolf Boldrewood, *Babes in the Bush* 279: 'a blaster ould rapparee like me.'; **1908** E.S. Sorenson, *The Squatter's Ward* 343: 'the look that Tiddy the Sergeant will put on him when he hears the rapparee has throttled himself.'

Sagart n. 'priest'. Also as **soggarth**. **1919** Marion Miller Knowles, *The Little Doctor* 49: he could never become one with them, like the "soggarths aroon" of the beautiful Isle of the Sea; **1973** Rev. Walter Ebsworth, *Pioneer Catholic Victoria* 76: There was universal grief in Portland when the kindly, zealous and beloved "soggarth" died; **1998** Kerry Murphy, *Kerry Murphy's Memoirs* 93: The story of the game is now history and is well told by a Kerry Sagart, Father Jim O'Connell of Tralee.

Sail éille n. 'a cudgel used in faction fighting in the 18th and 19th centuries'. As **shillelagh, shillalagh, shillalah, shillaley**. **1806** Marcus Clarke, 'Horace' in the Bush' in *Australian Tales and Sketches* 117: With that sprig of shillalagh; **1840** 'Frank the Poet', 'A Dialogue Between Two Hibernians at Botany Bay' in *Old Bush Songs* 30: The caravets, shillelagh and Ribbonman's pike; **1859** William Kelly, *Life in Victoria* 138: their intuitive skill in the use of the shillelagh; **1883** Edward M. Curr, *Recollections of Squatting in Victoria* 173: hit one of the boys ... a trifle too hard with the shillalah; **1897** Thomas Archer, *Recollections of a Rambling Life* 16: armed with a shillelagh; **1900** Rolf Boldrewood, *Babes in the Bush* 321: 'I think half a dozen shillelahs at once must be nearly as bad as a blackfellow's club'; **1901** Mrs T.R. Andrews, *Stephen Kyrle* 249: 'I will thin, wid me own shillelah; **1913** J.R. Houlding, *Christopher Cockle's Australian Experiences* 255: 'or a shillaley aythir'; **1946** J.H.M. Abbott, *Red O'Shaughenessy* 18: 'These guards invariably carry a large shillelagh.'; **1949** Ruth Park, *Poor Man's Orange* 11: you would have thought they had parked their shillelaghs in the porch but a minute before.

Saol n. 'life'. In phr. 'the bad life'. **1998** Thomas Keneally, *The Great Shame* 110: or simply an droch-Shaol the Bad Life, the Bad Times.

Sasanach n. 'Englishman', English'. In form **Sassenach**. **1919** J.H.M. Abbott, *The Governor's Man* 112: 'Not a Sassenach among them'; **1998** Thomas Keneally, *The Great Shame* 29: to ensure that they learned something of the Sassenach language – English.

Scailp n. 'fissure in a rock, a rude cabin'. Also as **scalp, scalpeen**. **1998** Thomas Keneally, *The Great Shame* 32: when crosses of rushes or straw were hung over any small out house or scalp that contained seed 114: or in scalpeens, holes dug in the ruins in a 'tumbled' house; **1999** Christopher Koch, *Out of Ireland* 351: sleeping in scalpeens; **1999** Jill Blee, *Brigid* 91: 'Some put up a bit of a scailpeen with whatever they could find'.

Sceilp n. 'slap, cut of whip or stick'. See also British dialect. In form **skelp**. **1948** Ruth Park, *The Harp in the South* 143: and skelping kids left and right.

Seachránaí n. 'wanderer'. As **shaughraun**. **1962** Frank Bruno, *Fury at Finnegan's Folly* 31: 'and him clingin' like a barnacle itself to his swag, the bould shaughraun'.

Seamróg n. 'three leafed small plant'. As **shamrock**. **1921** 'John O'Brien', 'St Patrick's Day' in *Around The Boree Log* 114: And the treasured bunch of shamrock; **1965** Leslie Haylen, *Big Red* 49: a shamrock in a cherished pot; **1999** David Foster, *In The New Country* 92: raised in the shamrock off the lime-rich soil.

Seanchaí n. 'storyteller'. In form **seanachie**. **1943** Miles Franklin *All That Swagger* 75: Old expirees casual labour, contributed tales that had descended from the seanachies and Bards of Tara's zenith.

Seoinín n. Literally, 'Little John (Bull)'. A derisory name for an Irishman who mimics English ways. In form Shoneen. **1921** 'John O'Brien', 'The Helping Hand' in *Around The Boree Log* 59: He'd lay the Shoneen by the heels. Glossed as: 'An over-smart would-be gentleman; a term of contempt.'; **1998** Thomas Keneally, *The Great Shame* 430: 'including the respectable loyal Shoneens'.

Síbín n. 'a place where drink is sold without a licence'. In forms **shebeen, sheebeen**. **1908** E.S. Sorenson, *The Squatter's Ward* 198: 'Shure it's not to a shebeen Oi'll be afther takin' her on the whay.'; **1946** J.H.M. Abbott, *Red O'Shaughenessy* 151: 'I've half a good mind for to roast th' pair o' ye alive an' bur-rn down this dir-rty, stinkin, sheebeen'; **1946** Katherine Susannah

Prichard, *The Roaring Nineties* 273: selling wild flowers in the pubs and shebeens; **1962** Frank Bruno, *Fury at Finnegan's Folly* 50: after a visit to the shebeen; **1996** David Malouf, *The Conversations at Curlew Creek* 166: one of the most isolated of the shebeens they visited; **1998** Thomas Keneally, *The Great Shame* 88: to other men in pubs and shebeens in Goulbourn; **1999** Jill Blee, *Brigid* 47: 'don't you be sneaking down to Pat Keane's shebeen'; **2000** Peter Carey, *True History of the Kelly Gang* 54: she were in the way of running a little shebeen.

Síle na gCíoch n. phr. 'Sheila of the Breasts. An obscene stone fertility fetish'. In form **Sheela na Gig**. **1991** Vincent Buckley, *Last Poems* 70: Sheela-na-Gig (Title).

Síoga n. 'fairies'. In form **shee**. **1945** William Carty, 'The Piper of Drimacoo' in *The Waves of Cool-a-vin* 9: And the Shee-folk merry making there.

Siúl v. 'walk'. In form **suibhail** in chorus of song 'Walk, walk, walk, oh darling! Walk peacefully and walk quietly'. **1962** Frank Bruno, *Fury at Finnegan's Folly* 50: 'Suibhail, suibhail, suibhail a ruin/ Suibhail go socar agus suibhail-ciuin.

Sláinte interj. 'health!' a toast. **1994** Tim Winton, *The Riders* 18: 'Cheers! Slainte'.

Sleán n. 'spade for cutting turf'. In form **slane**. **1996** David Malouf, *The Conversations at Curlew Creek* 155: They set their slanes against the wall.

Slibhín n. 'sly person'. As **sleveen**. **1978** Richard Butler, *Against The Wind* 29: 'Hold your tongue, you little sleveen!'.

Sliotaracha n. 'balls used in the game of hurling'. As **sliothars**. **1998** Kerry Murphy, *Kerry Murphy's Memoirs* 239: Jerseys, footballs and sliothars (hurling balls) are supplied.

Smidiríní n. 'fragments.' In form **smithereens**. **1888** Henry Lawson, 'A Wild Irishman' in *Henry Lawson Short Stories and Sketches* 191: 'broke the bottle to smithereens'.

Spailpín n. 'itinerant or seasonal labourer'. In forms **spalpeen, spawlpeen, shpalpeen, spilpeen**. **1840** Anonymous, 'Mrs O'Keefe's Adventures in Australia' in *Old Bush Songs* 63: 'You spalpeen', sis he; **1845** James Tucker, *Ralph Rashleigh* 119: 'My governmint min, to be shure, you shpalpeen'; **1847** Edward Landor, *The Bushman* 143: called to the young spalpeen to get out of that; **1849** Alexander Harris, *The Emigrant Family* 109: 'Let the spalpeen go wid it himself.'; **1859** William Kelly, *Life in Victoria* 279: Irish spalpeens are duped into working their passage; **1865** Ellen Davitt, *Force and Fraud* 37: 'And more shame for him, the spalpeen!' Glossed: from the Gaelic – a low or mean fellow; **1896** Marcus Clarke, 'Horace' in the Bush' in *Australian Tales and Sketches* 116: 'Mac, ye spalpeen'; **1908** E.S. Sorenson, *The Squatter's Ward* 265: 'The owld spalpeen niver 'lows me in there at all, at all.'; **1913** J.R. Houlding, *Christopher Cockle's Australian Experiences* 45: 'Bad manners to ye for a lot of squalin' spalpeens'; 1923 J.H.M. Abbott, *Sydney Cove* 156: 'ye white-livered spilpeen'; **1938** Xavier Herbert, *Capricornia* 187: 'take care of these poor spalpeens'; **1943** Miles Franklin, *All That Swagger* 3: 'I'll break the young spalpeen's back.'; **1946** J.H.M. Abbott, *Red O'Shaughenessy* 155: 'I bruk th' furniture a little bit an' piled it a top o' th' two spalpeens'; **1947** Frank Clune, *Ben Hall* 23: 'Come along ye spalpeens'; **1948** Ruth Park, *The Harp in the South* 82: 'great splaw-footed spalpeen'; **1960** Elizabeth O'Connor, *The Irishman* 6: 'She would scream abuse at them, calling them spalpeens and heretics; **1962** Frank Bruno, *Fury at Finnegan's Folly* 36: 'If we bury him, what's the matter wid some dirty spalpeen sayin' that ourselves murthered him.'; **1998** Thomas Keneally, *The Great Shame* 8: 'the very lowest in society, the spalpeens, in Irish 'penny-scythes, living on wasteland in the mountains or in bogs'.

Spéirbhean n. 'beautiful woman'. **1999** Christopher Koch, *Out of Ireland* 164: But this was a fairy: a spéir bhean, or sky woman.

Spideog n. 'robin'. In form **spiddogue**. **1996** David Malouf, *The Conversations at Curlew Creek* 166: 'Spiddogue, spiddogue, now swear on this book in your mouth'.

Spleodar n. 'cheerfulness, vivacity'. In forms **splather, splother**. **1921** 'John O'Brien', 'St Patrick's Day' in *Around The Boree Log* 114; And the 'splather' of a necktie only once a year paraded; **1928** Marion Miller Knowles, *Pretty Nan Hartigan* 209: 'Twas no big splother of a bouquet of flowers she carried'.

Spraoi n. 'prolonged drinking bout'. In form **spree**. **1853** Ellen Clancy, *A Lady's Visit to the Gold Diggings of Australia* 66: They were returning to Melbourne for a spree; **1865** Henry Kingsley, *The Hillyars and the Burtons* 203: I was lost in contemplation of such a gigantic spree; 1882 Mary Fortune, *The Fortunes of Mary Fortune* 77: Such a spree as was that night held around the doctor's insensible body; **1883** Edward M Curr, *Recollections of Squatting in Victoria* 174: the old convict custom of going to town once a year "to have a spree"; **1888** Henry Lawson, 'A Wild

Irishman' in *Short Stories and Sketches* 190: while he was on 'spree'; **1889** Rolf Boldrewood, *Robbery Under Arms* 79: The other chaps were wild for a spree; **1895** Henry Goldsmith, *Euancondit* 7: 'My mate went off on a spree'; **1898** Edward Dyson, 'The Golden Shanty' in *Below and On Top and Other Stories* 99: to revel in an occasional "spree"; **1908** E.S. Sorenson, *The Squatter's Ward* 33: 'So we reckoned on havin' a real good spree.'; **1926** Marion Miller Knowles, *Pierce O'Grady's Daughter* 230: 'he's a foul-mouthed brute when on a spree after a pay-out'; **1930** Henry Handel Richardson, *The Fortunes of Richard Mahony* 55: had profited by his absence to empty the cash box and go off on the spree; **1932** Jim McCarthur, *Pan's Clan* 131: 'To me he doesn't look like coming peacefully away for a spree at the present moment'; **1934** Brian Penton, *Landtakers* 210: 'He's out on the spree there this three weeks'; **1946** Katherine Susannah Prichard, *The Roaring Nineties* 65: nothing less than a champagne spree; **1948** Ruth Park, *The Harp in the South* 61: 'She felt sure that Hughie was going on a Christmas spree.'; **1954** 'John O'Brien', 'When the "Sut" Drops Down' in *The Parish of St Mel's* 48: And Brother Ted came home today to see his folk between the sprees; **1959** Mary Durack, *Kings in Grass Castles* 163: bragging, swaggering, fighting and coming together on lively sprees; **1965** Leslie Haylen, *Big Red* 3: Red's father had been on the spree for days now; **1966** Bill Beatty, *Tales of Old Australia* 97: a desire to shake of the effects of a heavy spree; **1997** Ann McGrath, 'Sexuality and Australian Identities' in *Creating Australia* 46: White men blew their earnings on a 'gin-spree' or orgy of alcohol and Aboriginal women; **1999** Kim Scott, *Benang* 221: When there was a spree, stay clear away. It was not safe.

Straoil n. v. In forms **sthreel, streel, sthreeling** 1. 'a slovenly woman, a slattern' **1921** 'John O'Brien' 'Josephine' in *Around The Boree Log* 96: That Norah O'Neill is a sthreel. Glossed as: Slattern; also spelt streel: **1930** Henry Handel Richardson, *The Fortunes of Richard Mahony* 681: 'Instead of being let streel around with his highty-tighty airs.'; **1943** Miles Franklin, *All That Swagger* 137: 'What ever has come to that Rafferty streel, another day or two wouldn't worsen it.'/ 'There's no need to be in a flurry over that streel; 2. 'to go about aimlessly'; **1845** James Tucker, *Ralph Rashleigh* 100: 'If you go sthreeling about looking for more wages. you shan't touch a sthraw of Jack Canavan's whate.'; **1946** Katherine Susannah Prichard, *The Roaring Nineties* 45: From the camps too, laughter streeled. 3. 'a string (of beads etc.)' **1946** Katherine Susannah Prichard, *The Roaring Nineties* 319: the sun was setting behind a streel of clouds.

Súil n. 'eye'. As **sool**. **1998** Kerry Murphy, Kerry Murphy's Memoirs 28: We fished for trout with a rod and what we called a 'sool' or eye, a little noose made from a cow's tail.

Taibhse n. 'ghost'. As **thavish**. **1945** William Carty, 'The Tinkers' in *The Waves of Cool-a-vin* 8: For thavish or Puca, they don't seem to care Glossed as: Thavish – a ghost.

Taithín n. 'fistful (of rushes)'. As **tageen**. **1943** Miles Franklin, *All That Swagger* 83: 'I've had no more than a tageen, and it a day past'.

Taoiseach n. 'Prime Minister'. **1991** Vincent Buckley, 'Hunger Strike' in *Last Poems* 55: from taoiseach to taoiseach; **1998** Joe O'Sullivan, *Letter to my Irish-Australian Grandchild* 80: For example in 1998 the Taoiseach (Irish prime minister) visited China on a trade mission.

Tinteán n. 'fireplace'. In phr. 'there's no place like home'. **1999** Christopher Koch, *Out of Ireland* 515: níl aon tinteán mar do thinteán féin. There's no hearth like your own hearth.

Tír na nÓg n. 'Land of Youth' in Irish mythology. As **Tir nan Og**. **1963** Criena Rohan, *Down By The Dockside* 49: 'like the old Irish used to say–Tir nan nOg, the Land of the Ever Young.'

Toice n. 'pert girl, hussy, a wench'. As diminutive **thuckeen**. **1921** 'John O'Brien', 'Josephine' in *Around The Boree Log* 64: This one has a thuckeen now to sweep and mind the door. Glossed as: Celtic for 'flapper'.

Tráithnín n. 'piece of straw', and so, anything worthless. In form **traneen**. **1845** James Tucker, *Ralph Rashleigh* 101: 'I'll not charge you a traneen for all you'll ate of the besht of good living'; **1900** Rolf Boldrewood, *Babes in the Bush* 225: 'As well him as me – not that I cared a traneen for my life.'; **1919** Marion Miller Knowles, *The Little Doctor* 35: 'I wouldn't give a thraneen for it'.

Tuigeann tú? phr. 'do you understand?'. As **thiggim-thu**. **1921** 'John O'Brien', 'Moryah' in *Around The Boree Log* 140: "Thiggim-thu, my Old Man, thiggim-thu?". Glossed as: 'Don't you understand?

Uillinn n. 'elbow '. **1999** Jill Blee, *Brigid* 21: tin whistles and uileann pipes.

Uisce Beatha n. 'whiskey'. Also as **uisge beatha**. **1978** Richard Butler, *Against The Wind* 29 'Uisce beatha', she said softly; **1998** Joe O'Sullivan, *Letters to my Irish-Australian Grandchild* 77: The word comes from uisge beatha literally 'water of life'; **1999** Christopher Koch, *Out of Ireland* 531: 'and drink uisce beatha!'; **2002** Jill Blee, *The Liberator's Birthday* 36: 'Uisce beatha'.

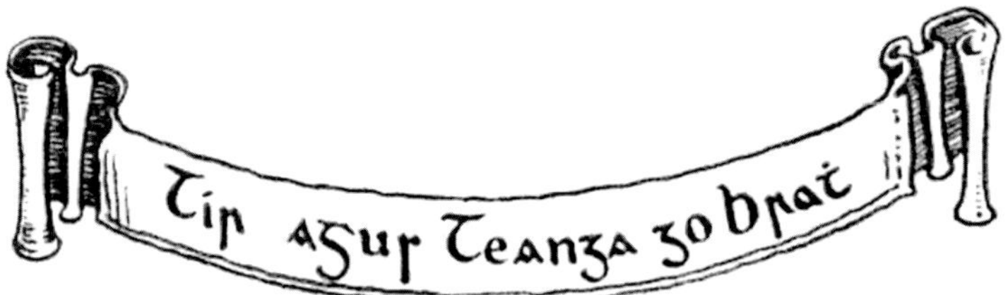
Tir agus Teanga go braṫ

BIBLIOGRAPHY

Primary Texts

Abbott, J.H.M. *The Governor's Man*, Melbourne: The Bookstall Company Pty Ltd, 1919.

Abbott, J.H.M. *Sydney Cove*, Sydney: Angus and Robertson, Ltd, 1923.

Abbott, J.H.M. *Red O'Shaughnessy*, Sydney: The Currawong Publishing Company, 1946.

Adams, Francis. *Australian Life*, London: Chapman and Hall Ltd, 1892.

Aldridge, James. *My Brother Tom*, London: Hamish Hamilton, 1966.

Andrews, Mrs T.R. *Stephen Kyrle*, Sydney: George Robertson and Co., 1901.

Ansted, Josephine. *The Son of the Bondswoman*, Sydney: Henry G Forster Publisher, 1925.

Archer, Thomas. *Recollections of a Rambling Life*, Brisbane: Boolarong Publications, 1988.

Beatty, Bill. *Tales of Old Australia* (1966), Sydney: Ure Smith Pty Ltd, 1969.

Becke, Louis. *The Adventures of Louis Blake* (1909), London: T Werner Laurie Ltd, 1913.

Blee, Jill. *Brigid*, Melbourne: Indra Publishing, 1996.

Blee, Jill. *The Liberator's Birthday*, Melbourne: Indra Publishing, 2002.

Boldrewood, Rolf. *Old Melbourne Memories* (1884), Melbourne: William Heinemann, 1969.

Boldrewood, Rolf. *Robbery Under Arms* (1888), St Lucia: University of Queensland Press, 1988.

Boldrewood, Rolf. *Babes in the Bush*, London: Macmillan and Co. Limited, 1900.

Boldrewood, Rolf. *The Miner's Right* (1890), London: Macmillan and Co. Ltd, 1903.

Bradshaw, Jack. *Highway Robbery Under Arms*, Sydney: The Worker Trustee, 1924.

Brent of Bin Bin. *Up The Country* (1928), Sydney: Angus and Robertson, 1968.

Bruce, Mary Grant. *Jim and Wally* (1916), Melbourne: Ward, Lock & Co. Limited, n.d.

Bruno, Frank. *Fury at Finnegan's Folly*, London: Robert Hale Limited, 1962.

Buckley, Vincent. *The Pattern*, Oxford: Oxford University Press, 1979.

Buckley, Vincent. *Memory Ireland*, Melbourne: Penguin Books, 1985.

Buckley, Vincent. *Last Poems*, Melbourne: McPhee Gribble, 1991.

Bunn, Anna Maria. *The Guardian* (1838), Canberra: Mulini Press, 1994.

Burke, Colleen Z and Vincent Woods. eds. *The Turning Wave: Poems and Songs of Irish Australia*, Sydney: Kardoorair Press Pty Ltd, 2001.

Burn, David. *The Bushrangers* (1829), Melbourne: Heinemann Educational Co., 1971.

Butler, Richard. *Against the Wind*, London: Severn House, 1978.

Carey, Peter. *True History of the Kelly Gang*, St Lucia: University of Queensland Press, 2001.

Carleton, William. *Stories from Carleton*, London: The Walter Scott Publishing Co., n.d.

Carty, William. *The Waves of Cool-a-vin*, Brisbane: The Co-operative Press, 1945.

Clancy, Ann. *The Wild Colonial Girl*, Sydney: Pan Macmillan, 1996.

Clancy, Laurie. *A Collapsible Man*, Melbourne: Outback Press, 1975.

Clark, Mavis Thorpe. *This Brown Land was Green*, London: William Heinemann Ltd, 1956.

Clarke, Marcus. *Old Tales of a Young Country* (1871), Sydney: Sydney University Press, 1972.

Clarke, Marcus. *For the Term of His Natural Life* (1874), Sydney: Reader's Digest Services Pty Ltd, 1987.

Clune, Frank. *Ben Hall* (1947), Melbourne: Pacific Books, 1963.

Collins, Tom. *Such is Life* (1903), Sydney: Angus and Robertson, 1968.

Crist, Alice Guerin. *When Rody Came to Ironbark*, Sydney: Cornstalk Publishing Company, 1927.

Curr, Edward M. *Recollections of Squatting in Victoria* (1883), Melbourne: Melbourne University Press 1965.

Dark, Eleanor. *Storm of Time*, Sydney: Angus and Robertson, 1980.

Davitt, Ellen. *Force and Fraud* (1865), Canberra: Mulini Press, 1993.

De Boos, Charles. *Mark Brown's Wife* (1871), Canberra: Mulini Press, 1992.

De Boos, Charles. *Fifty Years Ago* (1867), Canberra: Mulini Press, 1999.

De Paor, Louis. *Aimsir Bhreicneach,* Canberra: The Leros Press, 1993.

De Paor, Louis. *Gobán Cré is Cloch,* Melbourne: Black Pepper, 1996.

Durack, Mary. *Kings in Grass Castles* (1959), London: Transworld Publishing Ltd, 1971.

Dwyer, James Francis. *Leg-Irons On Wings*, Melbourne: Georgian House, n.d.

Fortune, Mary. *The Fortunes of Mary Fortune*, Melbourne: Penguin Books of Australia, 1989.

Foster, David. *In the New Country*, London: Fourth Estate Limited, 1999.

Fowler, Helen. *The Blazing Straw*, Sydney: Angus and Robertson, 1961.

Franklin, Miles. *All That Swagger,* Sydney: Angus and Robertson, 1943.

Furphy, Joseph. *Such is Life* (The Annotated), Sydney: Halstead Classics, 1999.

Gaskin, Catherine. *I Know My Love*, London: Collins, 1962.

Geoghan, Edward. *The Currency Lass* (1844), Sydney: Currency Press, 1976.

Gilmore, Mary. *Old Days: Old Ways*, Sydney: Angus and Robertson Ltd, 1934.

Goldsmith, Henry. *Euancondit,* London: Swan Sonnenschein and Co., 1895.

Harbinson, Jas E. *Poems*, Melbourne: 1902.

Harbinson, James. *Love Lyrics: And Other Poems*, Melbourne: The Poseidon Press, 1908.

Harbinson, James. *Selected Poems*, Melbourne: Southern Cross, 1919.

Hardie, J.J. *Pastoral Symphony,* Sydney: Angus and Robertson, 1947.

Harris, Alexander. *Settlers and Convicts* (1847), Melbourne: Melbourne University Press, 1964.

Harris, Alexander. *The Emigrant Family* (1849), Canberra, Australian National University Press, 1967.

Haylen, Leslie. *Big Red,* Sydney: Australasian Book Society, 1965.

Henderson, John. *Excursions and Adventures in New South Wales*, London: W Shoberl, 1851.

Herbert, Xavier. *Capricornia* (1938), Sydney: Angus and Robertson, 1971.

Heywood, B.A. *A Vacation Tour at the Antipodes,* London: Longman, Green, Longman, 1863.

Holburn Muir and Marjorie Pizer. eds. *Creeve Roe: Poetry by Victor Daly,* Sydney: The Pinchgut Press, 1947.

Hollingworth, Brian. *Maria Edgeworth's Irish Writing*, London: MacMillan Press, 1997.

Hosking, Rick. ed. *Robert Bruce Benbonuna*, Adelaide: Flinders University, 2002.

Houlding, John Richard. *Christopher Cockle's Australian Experiences,* Sydney: Angus and Robertson, 1913.

Howitt, William. *Land, Labour and Gold*, Kilmore: Lowden Publishing Company, 1972.

Kelly, William. *Life in Victoria*, Kilmore, Victoria: Lowden Publishing Co., 1977.

Keneally, Thomas. *Bring Lark and Heroes*, Melbourne: Cassell Australia, 1967.

Keneally, Thomas. *The Playmakers*, London: Serpentine Publishing Co. Pty Limited, 1987.

Keneally, Thomas. *Homebush Boy*, Melbourne: Minerva, 1995.

Keneally, Thomas. *The Great Shame*, Sydney: Random House, 1998.

Kingsley, Henry. *The Hillyers and the Burtons* (1865), Sydney: University of Sydney, 1973.

Knowles, Marion Miller. *Barbara Halliday,* Sydney: George Robertson and Co. Pty Ltd, 1896.

Knowles, Marion Miller. *Songs from the Hills*, Melbourne: Melville, Mullen and Slade, 1898.

Knowles, Marion Miller. *The Little Doctor,* Sydney: Pellegrini and Co., 1919.

Knowles, Marion Miller. *Pierce O'Grady's Daughter*, Sydney: Pellegrini and Co., 1926.

Knowles, Marion Miller. *Pretty Nan Hartigan*, Sydney: Pellegrini and Co., 1928.

Koch, Christopher. *The Boys in the Island* (1974), Sydney: Angus and Robertson, 1990.

Koch, Christopher. *Out of Ireland,* Sydney: Transworld Publishers, 1999.

Landor, Edward. *The Bushman: Or Life in a New Country* (1847), London: Johnson Reprint Co., 1970.

Laubenstein, William J. *The Emerald Whaler*, London: Andre Deutsch, 1961.

Lawson, Henry. *Short Stories and Sketches 1888-1922*, Sydney: Angus and Robertson, n.d.

Lawson, Henry. *Henry Lawson Short Stories and Sketches 1888-1922*, Sydney: Angus and Robertson, 1972.

Lawson, Henry. *A Camp-Fire Yarn,* Sydney: Lansdowne, 1984.

Lawson, Henry. *A Fantasy of Man,* Sydney: Lansdowne, 1984.

Lawson, Will and Hickey, Tom. *Moira of Green Hills*, Sydney: Australasian Publishing Company, 1950.

Mac Cártha, Fionán. *Amhráin Ó Dheireadh an Domhain*. Baile Átha Cliath (Dublin): Oifig an tSoláthair, 1953.

Malone, Rev. J.J. *Wild-Briar and Wattle Bloom,* Melbourne: Wm. P Linehan, 1914.

Malouf, David. *The Conversation at Curlew Creek*, London: Chatto and Windus, 1996.

Martin, Catherine. *An Australian Girl* (1890), London: Pandora Press, 1988.

Matthews, John Pengwerne. *Tradition in Exile*, Sydney: F W Cheshire, 1962.

McCarthur, Jim. *Pan's Clan,* Sydney: Deaton and Spencer, 1937.

McLean, Donald. *The Roaring Days*, London: Macmillan and Co., 1960.

Meehan, Michael. *The Salt of Broken Tears*, Sydney: Vintage, 1999.

Meredith, John and Rex Whalen. *Frank the Poet,* Melbourne: Red Rooster, 1979.

Miller, Marion. *Songs from the Hills*, Melbourne: Melville, Mullen and Slade, 1898.

Nelson, Kate and Dominica Nelson. eds. *Sweet Mothers, Sweet Maids*, Melbourne: Penguin Books, 1986.

Nichols, G.R. *Sydney Revels*, Sydney: Hawksley and Williamson, 1854.

Niland, D'Arcy. *The Shiralee* (1955), Sydney: Angus and Robertson, 1957.

Oakley, Barry. *A Salute to the Great McCarthy*, Melbourne: Penguin Books, 1971.

O'Brien, John. *The Parish of St Mel's*, Sydney: Angus and Robertson, 1954.

O'Brien, John. *Around The Boree Log*, Sydney: Angus and Robertson, 1961.

O'Connor, Elizabeth. *The Irishman*, Sydney: Angus & Robertson, 1960.

Park, Ruth. *The Harp in the South*, Sydney: Horwitz Publications, 1969.

Park, Ruth. *Poor Man's Orange*, Sydney: Horwitz Publications, 1969.

Paterson, A.B. *Outback Marriage*, Sydney: Angus and Robertson, 1906.

Paterson, A.B. *Three Elephant Power*, Sydney: Angus and Robertson, 1924.

Penton, Brian. *Landtakers*, Sydney: The Endeavour Press, 1934.

Prichard, Katherine Susannah. *The Roaring Nineties* (1946), Moscow: Foreign Language Publishing House, 1955.

Richardson, Henry Handel. *The Fortunes of Richard Mahony*, Sydney: The Discovery Press, 1968.

Rohan, Criena. *Down by the Dockside*, London: Victor Gollancz Ltd, 1963.

Savery, Henry. *The Hermit of Van Dieman's Land*, St Lucia: University of Queensland Press, 1964.

Scott, Kim. *Benang*, Fremantle: Fremantle Arts Centre Press, 1999.

Semmler, Clement. ed. *The World of 'Banjo' Paterson*, Sydney: Angus and Robertson, 1967.

Simpson, Helen. *Under Capricorn*, London: William Heinemann Ltd, 1937.

Sorenson, E.S. *The Squatter's Ward*, London: Hurst and Blackett Limited, 1908.

Stewart, Douglas and Nancy Keesing. eds. *Australian Bush Ballads*, Sydney: Angus and Robertson, 1962.

Stewart, Douglas and Nancy Keesing. *Old Bush Songs*, Sydney: Angus and Robertson, 1955.

Stone, Louis. *Jonah*, Sydney: Angus and Robertson, 1965.

The Spirit of the Nation: Or, Ballads and Songs by the Writers of "The Nation", Dublin: James Duffy & Sons, 1882.

Tucker, James. *Ralph Rashleigh*, Sydney: Angus and Robertson, The Discovery Press, 1953.

Tucker, James. *The Adventures of Ralph Rashleigh: A Penal Exile in Australia*, London: Jonathan Cape, 1929.

Vidal, Mary Theresa. *Bengala or Some Time Ago*, Sydney: New South Wales University Press, 1990.

Willmot, Eric. *Pemulwuy the Rainbow Warrior*, Sydney: Bantam Books, 1988.

Winstanley, Eliza. *For Her Natural Life*, Canberra: Mulini Press, 1992.
Winton, Tim. *The Riders*, Sydney: Pan Macmillan, 1994.

Newspapers, Journals and Websites

Aboriginal History 1.17, Canberra: 1993.
Aboriginal Art and Culture, Url: http://www.aboriginalart.com.au
The Age, (Melbourne).
The Advocate, (Melbourne).
An Claidheamh Soluis: The Gaelic Weekly (Dublin).
Auslit: Australian Literature Gateway: Url: http:www.auslit.edu.au
Canberra Sunday Times (Canberra)
Convicts to Australia, URL: http://www.convictcentral.com/index.html
The Gael, (Sydney) 1929.
The Galway Mercury, (Galway).
The Irish Australian (Sydney).
The Irish Times (Dublin) 20 April 1999.
Meanjin (Melbourne) 1979.
The Monitor (Sydney)
The Nation (Dublin).
On The Importance of Knowing French, www.utm.edu/~globeg/profren.shtml
The Oxford English Dictionary URL: www.oed.com 'revision program'.
The Southern Cross (Adelaide).
Táin (Melbourne).
Tuam Herald (Galway).

Secondary Sources

Ackland, Michael. ed. *The Penguin Book of Nineteenth Century Australian Literature,* Melbourne: Penguin Books, 1993

Acton, Charles. *Irish Music and Musicians*, Dublin: Eason and Son Ltd, 1978.

Amin, Shahid and Dipesh Chakrabarty. eds. *Subaltern Studies IX*, Delhi: Oxford University Press, 1996.

Amos, Keith. *The Fenians in Australia*, Kensington NSW: New South Wales University Press, 1988.

Anderson, Benedict. *Imagined Communities*, London: Verso, 1991.

Annear, Robyn. *Nothing but Gold: The Diggers of 1852*, Melbourne: The Test Publishing Company, 1999.

Archives Office of Tasmania, Hobart, ref. CON33/60, CON14/29, CON 18/37.

Argyle, Barry. 'James Tucker, Ralph Rashleigh' in *An Introduction to the Australian Novel 1830-1930*, Oxford: Clarendon Press, 1972: 60-83.

Ashcroft, Bill, Gareth Griffiths and Helen Tiffin. *The Empire Writes Back*, London: Routledge, 1989.

Ashcroft, Bill, Gareth Griffiths and Helen Tiffin. eds. *The Post-Colonial Studies Reader,* Routledge, London: 1995.

Ashcroft, Bill, Gareth Griffiths and Helen Tiffin. *Key Concepts in Post-Colonial Studies*, London: Routledge Press, 1998.

Atkinson, Alan. *The Europeans in Australia*, Melbourne: Oxford University Press, 1998.

Backhouse, James. *Extracts from the letters of James Backhouse*, London: Harvey and Danton, 1838.

Baker, Sydney J. *The Australian Language*, Melbourne: Sun Books Pty Ltd, 1970.

Bartley, J.O. *Teague, Shenkin and Sawney*, Cork: Cork University Press, 1954.

Beardsmore, Baetens Hugo. *Bilingualism: Basic Principles*, London: Tieto Ltd, 1982.

Beecher, Seán. *A Dictionary of Cork Slang*, Cork: The Collins Press, 1999.

Berger, Arthur. *Asa, An Anatomy of Humor*, New Jersey: Transaction Publishers, 1993.

Bernard, John. *Introduction to Linguistics: An Australian Perspective*, Sydney: Prentice Hall Australia, 1980.

Bhabha, Homi K. *The Location of Culture*, London: Routledge, 1994.

Bliss, Alan. *Spoken English in Ireland 1600–1749*, Dublin: Dolmen Press, 1969.

Bonwick, James. *Curious Facts of Old Colonial Days*, London: Sampson Low, Son and Marston, 1870.

Bourdieu, Pierre. *Language and Symbolic Power*, Cambridge, Mass: Harvard University Press, 1995.

Brewster, Anne. *Literary Formation, Post-colonialism, Nationalism*, Melbourne: Melbourne University Press, 1995.

Brissenden, Alan. ed. *Robbery Under Arms, essays and short stories*, Brisbane, University of Queensland Press, 1988.

Brody, Hugh. *Inishkillane: Change and Decline in the West of Ireland*, London: Pelican Books, 1974.

Brook, G.L. *Varieties of English*, London: MacMillan, 1973.

Brown, Christy. *Down All the Days*, London: World Books, 1971.

Bryson, John. ed. *Matthew Arnold Poetry and Prose*, London: Rupert Hart-Davis, 1954.

Buckley, Vincent. *Cutting Green Hay*, Melbourne: Penguin Books, 1983.

Buggy, Hugh. *Celtic Club: A Brief History 1887–1947*, Melbourne: n.p. 1947.

Bull, Philip, Chris McConville and Noel McLachlan. eds. *Irish Australian Studies Papers delivered at the Sixth Irish-Australian Conference July 1990*, Melbourne: La Trobe University, 1991.

Bull, Philip, Frances Devlin-Glass and Helen Doyle. eds. *Ireland and Australia 1798–1998*, Sydney: Crossing Press, 2000.

Bungman, Verity and Jenny Lee. eds. *Staining the Wattle*, Melbourne: Penguin Books, 1988.

Butler, Susan. *The Dinkum Dictionary*, Melbourne: Text Publishing, 2001.

Byrne, Desmond. *Australian Writers*, London: Richard Bentley and Son, 1896.

Cairns, David. *Writing Ireland: Colonialism, Nationalism and Culture*, Manchester: Manchester University Press, 1988.

Carleton, William. *Stories from Carleton*, London: The Walter Scott Publishing Co. Ltd, n.d.

Carter, Paul. *The Road to Botany Bay*, London: Faber and Faber, 1987.

Carty, James. *Ireland from Grattan's Parliament to the Great Famine*, Dublin: C J Fallon Limited, 1957.

Charney, Maurice. *Comedy High and Low*, New York: Peter Lang Publishing 1987.

Clark, James M. *The Vocabulary of Anglo-Irish*, St Gall: Folcroft Library Editions, 1974.

Clarke, Marcus. *Old Tales of a Young Country*, Sydney: Sydney University Press, 1972.

Cleary, P.S. *Australia's Debt to Irish Nation-Builders*, Sydney: Angus & Robertson, 1933.

Clyne, Michael. *Community Languages: The Australian Experience*, Cambridge: University of Cambridge, 1991.

Coldery, Barry. *Faith and Fatherland: The Christian Brothers and the Development of Irish Nationalism 1838–1921*, Dublin: Gill and MacMillan, 1988.

Collins, David. *An Account of the English Colony in New South Wales*, London: A.H. & A.W. Reed, 1975.

Connell, K.H. *Irish Peasant Society*, Dublin: Irish Academic Press, 1996.

Connell, R.W. and T.H. Irving. *Class Structure in Australian History*, Melbourne: Longman Cheshire Pty Ltd, 1986.

Connell, S.J. *Priests and People in PreFamine Ireland 1780–1845*, New York: Gill and MacMillan, St Martin's Press, n.d.

Conradh na Gaeilge: Registration Book (Dublin) 1895.

Corkery, Daniel. *The Hidden Ireland*, Dublin, M H Gill and Son Ltd, 1941.

Costello, Con. *Botany Bay*, Cork: The Mercier Press, 1987.

Coughlin, N. 'The Coming of the Irish to Victoria' in *Historical Studies*, Vol 12, no 45, October 1965.

Couzens, David. ed. *Foucault: A Critical Reader*, Oxford: Basil Blackwell, 1991.

Croghan, Martin J. 'Maria Edgeworth and the Tradition of Semiotics', in *International Aspects of Irish Literature*, Toshi Furomoto et al. eds, Gerrards Cross: Colin Smythe, 1996.

Crowley, Frank. *Colonial Australia*, Melbourne: Thomas Nelson Australia Pty Ltd, 1980.

Crystal, David. *Language Death*, Cambridge: University of Cambridge, 2000.

The Cunneen Family of Long Gully and Runnymeade, Melbourne: n.p. 1998.

Cunningham, Peter. *Two Years in New South Wales*, Sydney: Angus and Robertson, 1966.

Curtis, Edmund. *A History of Ireland*, London: Methuen & Co. Ltd, 1978.

Dale, R.W. *Impressions of Australia*, London: Hodder and Stoughton, 1889.

Davis, Richard. ed. *To Solitude Consigned: The Tasmanian Journal of William Smith O'Brien*, Sydney: Crossing Press, 1995.

Davis, R. 'The Great Shame' review in *Island* no. 78 Autumn 1999: 98–105.

Davis, Richard. *Revolutionary Imperialist William Smith O'Brien 1803–1864*, Sydney: Crossing Press, 1998.

Davis, Richard. *William Smith O'Brien: Ireland – 1848 – Tasmania*, Dublin: Geography Publications, 1989.

Davis, Richard, Jennifer Livett, Anne-Maree Whitaker and Peter Moore. eds. *Irish Australian Studies: Papers delivered at the Eight Irish-Australian Conference*, Hobart: University of Tasmania Press, 1995.

Day, David. *Claiming a Continent*, Sydney: Angus and Robertson, 1997.

De Izarra, Laura P.Z. 'The Irish Under The Southern Cross' in *Crop, Revista de rea Lingua e Literatures Inglesa e Norte-Americana*, No. 1, Sao Paulo: 1994.

Delbridge, Arthur. 'Australian English' in *The Penguin New Literary History of Australia*, Melbourne: Penguin Books Australia, 1988.

Derringcourt, William. *Old Convict Days* (1899), Melbourne: Penguin Books Australia Ltd, 1975.

Dineen, Patrick Rev. *Foclóir Gaedilge*, Dublin: M.H. Gill and Son Ltd, 1904.

Dixon, R.M., W.S. Ramson and Mandy Thomas. eds. *Australian Aboriginal Words in English*, Melbourne: Oxford University Press, 1990.

Dolan, Jay. *The Immigrant Church: New York's Irish and German Catholics 1815–1865*, Baltimore: Johns Hopkins University, 1975.

Dolan, Terence Patrick. *A Dictionary of Hiberno-English*, Dublin: Gill and Macmillan, 1999

Dorian, Nancy C. *Language Death*, Philadelphia: University of Pennsylvania, 1981.

Duggan, G.C. *The Stage Irishman*, London: Benjamin Blom, 1969.

During, Simon. ed. *The Cultural Studies Reader*, London: Routledge, 1995.

Dutton, Geoffrey. ed. *The Literature of Australia*, Melbourne: Penguin Books, 1964.

Dunderdale, George. *The Book of the Bush*, Melbourne: Penguin Books, 1973.

Dutton, Geoffrey. *The Literature of Australia*, Melbourne: Penguin Books, 1964.

Eagleson, Robert D. *Australianisms in Early Migrant Handbooks: 1827–1830: Occasional Paper No. 4*, Sydney: The University of Sydney, 1965.

Eagleton, Terry. *Literary Theory*, Oxford: Basil Blackwell Ltd, 1988.

Ebsworth, Rev. Walter. *Pioneer Catholic Victoria*, Melbourne: The Polding Press, 1973.

Edgeworth, Maria. *Castle Rackrent*, London: J.M. Dent & Sons Ltd, 1960.

English Today, 63, vol. 16 no. 3 July 2000.

Evans, Geraint, Bernard Martin and Jonathon M. Wooding. eds., *Origins and Revivals: Proceedings of the First Australian Conference of Celtic Studies*, Sydney: Centre for Celtic Studies, University of Sydney, 2000.

Edwards, J.R. *The Irish Language: An Annotated Bibliography of Sociolinguistic Publications 1772–1982*, New York: Garland, 1983.

Éire-Ireland, New Jersey: Irish American Cultural Institute, Summer 1995.

Elliott, Brian and Adrian Mitchell. *Bards in the Wilderness*, Sydney: Thomas Nelson, 1970.

English World Wide vol. 12.2, Philadelphia: John Benjamins North America Inc., 1991.

Evans, Estan. *Irish Folk Ways*, London: Routledge and Kegan Paul, 1957.

Fanning, Charles. *The Irish Voice in America*, Lexington: The University Press of Kentucky, 1990.

Finnegan, Frances. *Poverty and Prejudice*, Cork: Cork University Press, 1982.

Fitzpatrick, D. *Irish Emigration 1801–1921*, Dublin: Dundalgan Press, 1985.

Fitzpatrick, David. *Oceans of Consolation*, Melbourne: University Press, 1995.

Fletcher, Brian. *Colonial Australia Before 1850*, Sydney: Thomas Nelson Australia, 1986.

Foley, Tadgh and Fiona Batemen. eds. *Irish-Australian Studies: Papers Delivered at the Ninth Irish-Australian Conference*, Galway, 1997, Sydney: Crossing Press, 2000.

Foster, R.F. *Modern Ireland 1600–1972*, London: Allen Lane The Penguin Press, 1988.

Roy Foster. ed. *The Oxford Illustrated History of Ireland*, London: Guild Publishing, 1989.

Fowler, Frank. *Southern Lights and Shadows* (1859), Sydney: Sydney University Press, 1975.

Fréine, Seán De. *The Great Silence*, Dublin: Foilseacháin Náisiúnta Teoranta, 1965.

Furomoto, Toshu, George Hughes, Chizuko Inous, James McElwain, Peter MCMillan and Tetsuro Sano eds. *International Aspects of Irish Literature*, London: Colin Smythe, 1996.

Gibson. Ross. *South of the West, Postcolonialism and the Narrative Construction of Australia*, Indianapolis: Indiana University Press, 1992.

Graham, Col, Perry McIntyre and Anne-Maree Whitaker. eds. *The Voyage of the Ship Friendship*, Sydney: PR Ireland, 2000.

Gray, Peter. *The Irish Famine*, London: Thames and Hudson, 1997.

Gra,. Tony. *Saint Patrick's People*, London: Warner Books, 1997.

Green H.M. *A History of Australian Literature*, Sydney: Angus and Robertson 1966.

Greet, Martin. 'The Irish and Fenianism in South Australia during 1868', PhD Thesis, The Flinders University of South Australia 1987.

Grimes, Seamus and Gearóid Ó Tuathaigh. eds. *The Irish-Australian Connection: An Caidreamh Gael-Astrálach*, Dublin: Academic Press, 1989.

Gudykunst, William B. ed. *Language and Ethnic Identity*, Philadelphia: Multilingual Matters Ltd, 1988.

Guerin, Wilfred L., Earle Labor, Lee Morgan, C. Jeanne, R. Reesman, and John Willingham. *A Handbook of Critical Approaches to Literature*, Fourth Edition, Oxford: Oxford University Press, 1999.

Haley, Martin. *Poems and Preface*, Brisbane: W R Smith & Paterson Pty Ltd, 1936.

Hall, Rodney. *The Second Bridegroom*, Sydney: McPhee Gribble, 1991.

Hamel, Van A.G. 'On Anglo-Irish Syntax', in *Englishe Studien* XLV, 1912.

Hamer, Clive. 'Fifty Years Ago' – an Overlooked Novel' in *Southerly* vol. 18 no. 1 1957: 41–44.

Harasym, Sarah. ed. *The Post-Colonial Critic*, London: Routledge, 1990.

Harmer, Maurice. ed. *Fenians and Fenianism*, Dublin: Scepter Publishers, 1986.

Harris, Alexander. *The Secrets of Alexander Harris*, Sydney: Angus and Robertson, 1961.

Hayden, Mary and Marcus Hartog. 'The Irish Dialect of English: Its Origins and Vocabulary', in *Fortnightly Review* LXXXV (1909): 775–785, 933–947.

Healy, James N. ed. *The Mercier Book of Old Irish Street Ballads*, Cork: The Mercier Press, 1969.

Healy, J. 'The Convict and the Aborigine: The Quest for Freedom in 'Ralph Rashleigh' in *Australian Literary Studies* vol. 3 no. 4 October 1968: 243–253.

Henricksen, Noel. 'Vexilla Regis Prodeunt: Myth and Allusion in Out of Ireland' in *Australian Literary Studies*, vol. 20 no. 1 May 2001: 33–48.

Herford, C.H, Percy and Evelyn Simpson. eds. *Ben Jonson*, Oxford: Clarendon Press, 1963.

Hergenhan, Laurie. 'Ralph Rashleigh: A Convict Dream' in *Australian Literary Studies* vol. 7 no. 3 May 1976: 279–293.

Hergenhan, Laurie. *Unnatural Lives: Studies in Australian Fiction about the Convicts*, St Lucia, Qld: University of Queensland Press, 1993.

Historical Records of Australia Series 1 Vol. 11 1797–1800, Sydney: The Library Committee of the Commonwealth Parliament, 1914.

Historical Studies, Melbourne: University of Melbourne, Vol. 12 no. 45 October 1965.

Hodge, Bob and Vijay Mishra. *Dark Side of the Dream*, Sydney: Allen and Unwin, 1991.

Hogan, J.F. *The Irish in Australia*, London: Ward & Downey, 1887.

Hogan, Jeremiah J. *The English Language in Ireland* (1927), Maryland: McGrath Publishing Company, 1970.

Hollingworth, Brian. *Maria Edgeworth's Irish Writing*, London: MacMillan Press, 1997.

Holt, Joseph. *Life of General Joseph Holt*, Sydney: Mitchell Library CY 17 A.2024, 1827.

Holt, Joseph. *A Rum Story: The Adventures of Joseph Holt*, Sydney: Kangaroo Press, 1988.

Horne, Donald. *The Lucky Country*, Melbourne: Penguin Books, 1967.

Horvath, Barbara M. *Variations in Australian English*, Canberra: Australian National University Press, 1966.

Horvath, Barbara and Paul Vaughan. *Community Languages*, Avon: Multilingual Matters, 1991.

Houston, Cecil J., and William J. Smith. *Irish Emigration and Canadian Settlement: Patterns, Links and Letters*, Toronto: University of Toronto Press, 1990.

Hudson, Wayne and Geoffrey Bolton. eds. *Creating Australia*, s., Sydney: Allen and Unwin, 1997.

Hughes, Robert. *The Fatal Shore*, London: William Collins Sons and Co. Ltd, 1987.

Hughes, Joan. ed. *Australian Words and Their Origins*, Melbourne: Oxford University Press, 1989.

Hyde, Douglas. *A Literary History of Ireland*, London: T Fisher Unwin, 1901.

Ignatiev, Noel. *How The Irish Became White*, New York: Routledge, 1995.

Ihde, Thomas W. ed. *The Irish Language in the United States*, Westport, Connecticut: Bergin and Garvey, 1994.

Ingham, S.M. *Enterprising Migrants*, Melbourne: The Hawthorn Press, 1975.

Irvin, Eric. 'Australia's First Dramatists', in *Australian Literary Studies*, Vol 4 no. 1 May 1969.

Jeffares, A. Norman. *Anglo-Irish Literature*, New York: Schoken Books, 1982.

Joyce, James. *A Portrait of the Artist as a Young Man*, London: Granada Publishing, 1979.

Joyce, P.W. *English as We Speak it in Ireland*, Dublin: Wolfhound Press, 1988.

Jackson, T.A. *Ireland Her Own* (1970), London: Lawrence & Wishart, 1991.

Johansen, Lenie. *The Penguin Book of Australian Slang*, Melbourne: Penguin Books, 1996.

Jones, Charles. *A Language Suppressed*, Edinburgh: John Donald, 1995.

Kavanagh, Paul and Peter Kuch. 'Scored for the Voice: An Interview with Vincent Buckley', in *Southerly*, no. 3 1987.

Kelly, Sister Mary Edith. *The Irishman in the English Novel of the Nineteenth Century*, Washington: The Catholic University of America, 1939.

Kennedy, Conan. ed. *Irish Language Ireland*, Killala, Co. Mayo: Morrigan Books, 1998.

Kenny, Kevin. *Making Sense of the Molly Maguires*, New York: Oxford University Press, 1998.

Kiberd, Declan. *Inventing Ireland*, Cambridge, Mass: Harvard University Press, 1995.

Kiddle, Margaret. *Men of Yesterday*, Melbourne: Melbourne University Press, 1961.

Kiernan, Colm. ed. *Australia and Ireland 1788–1988 Bicentenary Essays*, Sydney: Angus and Robertson, 1984.

Kiernan, T.J. *The Irish Exiles in Australia*, Dublin: Clonmore and Reynolds Ltd, 1954.

Kiernan, T.J. *Transportation from Ireland to Sydney*, Canberra: n.p. 1954.

Kramsch, Claire. *Language and Culture*, Oxford: Oxford University Press, 1998.

Lang, John. *Botany Bay*, Hobart: J Walch and Sons Pty Ltd, 1932.

Langker, R. *Flash in New South Wales: Occasional Paper No. 18*, Sydney: The University of Sydney, 1980.

Laxton, Edward. *The Famine Ships*, London: Bloomsbury, 1996.

Lea-Scarlett, Errol. *Queanbeyan District and People* (1932), Queanbeyan NSW: Queanbeyan Municipal Council, 1968.

Leerssen, Joep. *Mere Irish and Fíor-Ghael*, Cork: Cork University Press, 1996.

Leerssen, Joep. *Rembrance and Imagination*, Notre Dame: University of Notre Dame Press, 1997.

Livingston, Ken. *Nothing but the Same Old Story: The Roots of Anti-Irish Racism*, Nottingham: The Russell Press Ltd, 1986.

Lloyd, David. 'Discussion Outside History: Irish New Histories and the 'Subalternity Effect' in *Subaltern Studies IX*, Shahid Amin and Dipesh Chakrabarty eds., Delhi: Oxford University Press, 1996.

Lonergan, Dymphna. 'The Significance of Irish Gaelic in Anglo-Irish Writing 1800-1989', MA Thesis, Flinders University of South Australia, 1994.

Lynham, E.W. *The Irish Character in Print 1571–1923*, Shannon: Irish University Press, 1969.

Lyons, F.S. *Ireland Since the Famine*, London: The Fontana Press, 1985.

MacDonagh, Oliver and W.F. Mandle. eds. *Irish-Australian Studies: Papers delivered at the Fifth Irish-Australian Conference*, Canberra: Australian National University, 1989.

Mclaughlin, Trevor. ed. *Irish Women in Colonial Australia*, Sydney: Allen & Unwin, 1998.

MacLennan, Malcolm. *Gaelic Dictionary*, Edinburgh: Acair Press, 1996.

Maguire, Gabrielle. *Our Own Language*, Clevedon U.K., Multilingual Matters, 1991.

McArthur, Tom. ed. *The Oxford Companion to the English Language*, Oxford: Oxford University Press, 1992.

McCrum, Robert, William Cran and Robert McNeil. *The Story of English*, London: Faber and Faber, 1989.

MacDonagh, Oliver, W.F. Mandle and Pauric Travers. eds. *Irish Culture and Nationalism: 1750–1950*, London: The MacMillan Press, 1983.

MacDonagh, Oliver and W.F. Mandle. eds. *Ireland and Irish-Australia*, Sydney: Croom Helm Australia Pty Ltd, 1986.

McDougall, J.K. *The Trend of the Ages*, Melbourne: Labor Call Print, 1922.

McDowell, R.E. ed. *Social Life in Ireland 1800–1845*, Dublin: Three Candles, 1963.

McLaren, John. *Australian Literature, An Historical Introduction*, Melbourne: Longman Cheshire Pty, 1989.

McLachlan, Noel. ed. *The Memoirs of James Hardy Vaux*, London: Heinemann, 1964.

Mclaughlin, Trevor. ed. *Irish Women in Colonial Australia*, Sydney: Allen & Unwin, 1998.

Mecham, Frank. *"John O'Brien" and the Boree Log*, Sydney: Angus and Robertson, 1981.

Mecham, Frank. *Boree Log: Early Australian History in the Poems of "John O'Brien"*, Brisbane: Leader Press, 1985.

Meredith, John and Rex Whalen. *Frank the Poet*, Melbourne: Red Rooster, 1979.

Meredith, Louisa Anne. *Notes and Sketches of New South Wales* (1844), London: John Murray, n.d.

Miller, Kerby. *Emigrants and Exiles*, Oxford: Oxford University Press, 1985.

Mitchell, A.G. *The Australian Accent: Fifth Annual Report of the Australian Humanities Research Council*, Adelaide: n.p. 1961.

Mitchel, John. *Jail Journal*, Dublin: M.H.Gill & Son, Ltd, (1854) 1960.

Moore, Bruce. *Gold! Gold! Gold!*, Oxford: Oxford University Press, 1999.

Moore, Bruce. ed. *The Australian Oxford Dictionary*, Canberra: Australian National Dictionary Centre, 2000.

Moran, Cardinal. *History of the Catholic Church in Australasia*, Sydney: Oceanic Publishing Co. Ltd, n.d.

Morris, E.E. Austral English, *A Dictionary of Australian Words, Phrases and Usages*, London: Macmillan and Co. Limited, 1898.

Mortlock, J.F. *Experiences of a Convict*, Sydney: Sydney University Press, 1965.

Murphy, Frank. *The Bog Irish*, Melbourne: Penguin Books, 1987.

Murphy, Kerry. *Kerry Murphy's Memoirs: The Diaries of an Irish Immigrant*, Sydney: Walla Walla Press, 1998.

National Library of Ireland, 'Images of Erin in the Age of Parnell', leaflet, 2001.

O'Brien, Eris. *Life and Letters of Archpriest John Joseph Therry*, Sydney: Angus and Robertson, 1922.

'O'Brien, John'. *The Men of '38 and other Pioneer Priests*, Kilmore: Lowden Publishing Co., 1975.

O'Brien, John and Pauric Travers. eds. *The Irish Emigrant Experience in Australia*, Dublin: Poolbeg Press, 1991.

Ó Cuív, Brian. *Irish Dialects and Irish-speaking Districts*, Dublin: Institute of Advanced Studies, 1951.

Ó Cuív, Brian. ed. *A View of the Irish Language*, Dublin: The Stationery Office, 1969.

Ó Dónaill, Niall. *Foclóir Gaeilge-Béarla*, Baile Átha Cliath (Dublin): Oifig an tSoláthair, 1977.

O'Dowd, Anne. *Spalpeens and Tattie Hokers*, Dublin: Irish Academic Press, 1991.

Ó Donnchadha, Tadhg. *Féilscríbhinn Torna*, Cork: University of Cork Press, 1947.

O'Farrell, Patrick. *The Catholic Church and Community in Australia*, Melbourne: Thomas Nelson (Australia) Limited, 1977.

O'Farrell, Patrick. *The Catholic Church and Community*, Sydney: New South Wales University Press, 1985.

O'Farrell, Patrick. *The Irish in Australia*, Sydney: New South Wales University Press, 1987.

O'Farrell, Patrick. *Vanishing Kingdoms*, Sydney: New South Wales University Press, 1990.

O'Farrell, Patrick. *The Irish in Australia*, Sydney: New South Wales University Press, 2000.

Óg, Seán & Mánus Ó Baoill. eds. *Ceolta Gael*, Dublin: Mercier Press, 1975.

Ó Huallachán, Colmán. *The Irish and Irish*, Dublin: Assisi Press, 1994.

O'Leary, Peter. *My Own Story*, Cork: The Mercier Press, 1970.

Ó Luineacháin, Dáithí. *Ó Ghlíomáil go Giniúint: Foclóir na Collaíochta*, Baile Átha Cliath (Dublin): Coiscéim, 1997.

O'Mahony, Christopher, and Valerie Thompson. *Poverty to Promise*, Sydney: Crossing Press, 1994.

Ó Muirithe, Diarmaid. *A Seat Behind the Coachman*, Dublin: Four Courts Press, 1972.

Ó Muirithe Diarmaid. ed. *The English Language in Ireland*, Dublin: The Mercier Press, 1977.

Ó Muirithe, Diarmaid. *A Dictionary of Anglo-Irish*, Dublin: Four Courts Press, 1996.

Ó Murchu, Máirtín. *The Irish Language*, Dublin: The Department of Foreign Affairs and Bord na Gaeilge, 1985.

O'Neill, Timothy. *Life and Tradition in Rural Ireland*, London: J.M. Dent & Sons Ltd, 1977.

Oppenheim, Helen. 'The Author of The Hibernian Father: An Early Colonial Playwright, in *Australian Literary Studies*, Vol 2 no. 4 December 1966.

Ó Siadhail, Mícheál. *Modern Irish*, Cambridge: Cambridge University Press, 1989.

O'Sullivan, Joe. *Echoes of Ireland: Letters to my Irish-Australian Grandchild*, Perth: Centre for Irish Studies, Murdoch University, 1998.

O'Sullivan, Patrick. ed. *The Irish in the New Communities*, Leicester: Leicester University Press, 1992.

O'Sullivan, Vincent. 'Singing Mastery: The Poetics of Vincent Buckley', in *Westerly*, no. 2, vol 34 June 1989.

Ó Tuathaigh, Gearóid. *Ireland Before the Famine*, Dublin: Gill and MacMillan, 1972.

Partington, Geoffrey. *The Australian Nation Its British and Irish Roots*, Melbourne: Australian Scholarly Publishing, 1994.

Partridge, Eric, and John W. Clark. *British and American English since 1900*, London: Andrew Dakers Limited, 1951.

Partridge, Eric. *A Dictionary of Slang and Unconventional English*, London: Routledge and Kegan Paul, 1984.

Pelan, Rebecca. ed. *Irish-Australian Studies: Papers delivered at the Seventh Irish-Australian Conference July 1993*, Sydney: Crossing Press, 1994.

Pelan, Rebecca. 'The Great Shame' review in *Overland* no. 158 Autumn 2000: 115-115.

Perkins, Harold. *The Convict Priests*, Melbourne: Thistle Press Pty, Ltd, n.d.

Petersen, Kirsten Holt and Anna Rutherford. eds. *Displaced Persons*, Sydney: Kangaroo Press, 1988.

Pierce, Peter. *Australian Melodramas*, St Lucia: University of Queensland Press, 1995.

The Pioneering Collins. Canberra: Canberra Publishing and Printing Co., n.d.

Praite, R. and J.C. Tolley. *Place Names of South Australia*, Sydney: Rigby Limited, 1970.

Pyles, Thomas. *The Origins and Development of the English Language*, New York: Harcourt Brace Jovanovich, Inc., 1971.

Ramson, W.S. *Commonwealth Literary Fund Lectures 1963: Australian English*, Canberra: Australian National University. 1963.

Ramson, W.S. *Australian English: An Historical Study of the Vocabulary 1788-1895*, Canberra: Australian National University Press, 1966.

Ramson, W.S. ed. *Australian National Dictionary*, Melbourne: Oxford University Press, 1988.

Reece, Bob. ed. *Exiles From Erin*, London: MacMillan Academic and Professional Ltd,1991.

Reece, Bob. *Irish Convict Lives*, Sydney: Crossing Press, 1993.

Reece, Bob. 'Green Among the Gold' in *Australia in the World*, Don Grant and Graham Seal. eds. Perth: Black Swan Press, 1994.

Reece, Bob. *The Origins of Irish Convict Transportation To New South Wales*, New York: Palgrave, 2001.

Reece, R.H.W. *Aborigines and Colonists*, Sydney: Sydney University Press, 1974.

Richards, Eric. 'Irish life and progress in colonial South Australia', in *Irish Historical Studies*, Dublin: Vol. XXV11 No. 107, May 1991.

Rickard, John. *Australia a Cultural History*, London: Longman, 1988.

Rivkin, Julie and Michael Ryan. *Literary Theory: An Anthology*, Oxford: Blackwell Publishers Inc. 1998.

Robson, L.L. *The Convict Settlers in Australia*, Melbourne: Melbourne University Press, 1976.

Roderick, Colin. ed. *Henry Lawson Criticism*, Sydney: Angus and Robertson, 1972.

Rosenberg, Jerome H. 'Narrative Perspectives and Cultural History in Robbery Under Arms', in *Australian Literary Studies*, Vol 6 no. 1, Hobart: University of Tasmania, 1973.

Rowcroft, Charles. *The Australian-Crusoes; or, The Adventures of an English Settler and his family*, (1843), Philadelphia: Ellis P Hazard, n.d.

Rushdie, Salman. *Imaginary Homelands*, London: Granta Books, 1991.

Russell, A. *A Tour through the Australian Colonies*, Glasgow: David Robertson, 1840.

Said, Edward W. *Culture and Imperialism*, New York: Vintage Books, 1994.

Saunders, Ian. *Open Texts, Partial Maps*, Perth: University of Western Australia, 1993.

Schlauch, Margaret. *The English Language in Modern Times (since 1400)*, London: Oxford University Press, 1964.

Schaffeld, Robert. 'The Making of a Myth' in *Writing in Australia: perceptions of Australia in its historical and cultural context: a series of lectures given at Hamburn University on the occasion of 1st Festival of Australian Literature*, Gerd Dose and Bettina Keil eds., n.p., 1995,

Serjeantson, Mary S. *A History of Foreign Words in English*, London: Routledge and Kegan Paul, 1962.

Shapiro, Michael. ed. *Language and Politics*, New York: New York University Press, 1984.

Shaw Sailer, Susan. ed. *Representing Ireland: Gender, Class, Nationality*, Gainsville: University of Florida Press, 1997.

Simmons, Kathleen. "The Ireland Inside Me": Irish Cultural Memory in Australian Writing Since World War 11', PhD Thesis, University of Queensland, 1996.

Simpson, J.A. and E.S.C. Weiner. eds. *The Oxford English Dictionary*, Second Edition, Oxford: Clarendon Press, 1989.

Smith, F.B. ed. *Ireland England and Australia*, Canberra: Australian National University Press, 1990.

Southerwood, W.T. *Lonely Shepherd in Van Diemen's Land*, Launceston, Stella Maris Books, 1988.

The Spirit of the Nation: Ballads and Songs by Writers of "The Nation", James Duffy and Co., Dublin: 1898.

Strang, Barbara M.H. *A History of English*, London: Methuen & Co. Ltd, 1970.

Swift, Jonathan. *A Proposal for Correcting the English Tongue Polite Conversations, etc.*, Oxford: Basil Blackwell, 1964.

Swift, Roger and Sheridan Gilley. eds. *The Irish in Britain, 1815–1939,* London: Pinter Publishers, 1989.

The Sydney Gazette and New South Wales Advertiser, Sydney: Angus and Robertson, 1964.

Terry, Michael. *Across Unknown Australia*, London: Herbert Jenkins Limited, 1926.

Thiebergers, Nick and William McGregor. eds. *Macquarie Aboriginal Words*, Sydney: The Macquarie Library Pty Ltd, 1999.

Tiffin, Chris and Alan Lawson. ed. *De-Scribing Empire*, London: Routledge, 1994.

Thompson, A.K. 'The Poetry of Vincent Buckley' in *Meanjin*, no, 118, vol. XXV11 Spring 1969.

Todd, Loreto. *The Language of Irish Literature*, London: Macmillan Education, 1989.

Trudgill, Peter. ed. *Language in the British Isles*, Cambridge: Cambridge University Press, 1984.

Troy, Jakelin. *Australian Aboriginal Contact with the English Language in New South Wales 1788–1845*, Pacific Linguistic Series B-no 103, Canberra: Australian National University, 1990.

Trudgill, Peter. *Sociolinguistics*, Melbourne: Penguin Books, 1983.

Truninger, Annelise. *Paddy and the Paycock*, Bern: A. Francke A.G. Verlag Bern, 1976.

Ullathorne, Archbishop. *The Autobiography of Archbishop Ullathorne*, London: Burns & Oates Limited, n.d.

Ullathorne, W. *The Catholic Mission in Australasia* (1837), Adelaide: Libraries Board of South Australia, 1963.

Waldersee, James. *Catholic Society in New South Wales 1788–1860*, Sydney: Sydney University Press, 1974.

Wannan, Bill. ed. *The Wearing of the Green*, Melbourne: Lansdowne Press, 1965.

Ward, Peter. 'Down by the Dockside' review in *Australian Book Review* vol. 3 no. 4 February 1964: 90.

Ward, Russell. *The Australian Legend*, Melbourne: Oxford University Press, 1978.

Ward, Russell. *Finding Australia*, Melbourne: Heinemann Educational Australia, 1987.

Watson, Chris. 'Around the Boree Log and Australian Irish Identity' paper given at the Through Irish Eyes conference, Ballarat, December 1999.

Welch, Robert. ed. *The Oxford Companion to Irish Literature*, Oxford: Clarendon Press, 1996.

Whitaker, Anne-Maree. *Unfinished Revolution: United Irishmen in New South Wales 1800–1810*, Sydney: Crossing Press, 1994.

Whitaker, Anne-Maree. 'Lexicography as Cultural Genocide: The Irish Influence on the Australian Language' in *Australian Celtic Journal* no. 6, Sydney: The Celtic Council of Australian 2001: 65.

Wierzbicka, Anna. *Understanding Cultures through their Key Words*, Oxford: Oxford University Press, 1997.

Wilde, H. William, Joy Hooton and Barry Andrews. *The Oxford Companion to Australian Literature*, Melbourne: Oxford University Press, 1985.

Wilkes, G.A. *Exploring Australian English*, Sydney: ABC Books, 1993.

Wilkes, G.A. *A Dictionary of Australian Colloquialisms*, Oxford: Oxford University Press, 1996.

Williams, John. *Ordered To The Island*, Sydney: Crossing Press, 1994.

Wright, Joseph. *The English Dialect Dictionary*, Oxford: Oxford University Press, 1961.

Zimmermann, Georges-Denis. *Songs of Irish Rebellion*, Hatboro Penn: Folklore Associates, Inc., 1967.

INDEX

I

J

K

L

M

N

O

W

Y

Lythrum Press

1st floor, 128 Hindley Street
Adelaide
South Australia 5000

Telephone: (08) 8415 5150

www.lythrumpress.com.au